ORDER

IN THE

ORDER

By

TANYA RICE

Table Of Contents

Acknowledgments

I would like to thank everyone who motivated and encouraged me to write this Study Session, y'all scary chumps asked me not to mention your names but I appreciate y'all anyway. Special thanks to Past Grand Matron Kia Lewis and Past Worthy Matron Carmen Chaisson.

To my mother, my guardian angel, Mary M Rice, I FINALLY reached the minimum age to become a member of the Order of the Eastern Star. LoL

You left me in this world to fight these battles alone. I guess The Most High needed you to be a soldier on his battlefield more than I needed you on Earth. I can't thank you enough for the good stern upbringing and for instilling the importance of a good education in me. I'm no Einstein but you put me in a position where I can hold my own.

You are greatly missed but not a day goes by that I don't think of you. I felt your presence as I wrote this study session and I pray that I made you proud. Please continue to protect me in your absence though you will always be in my presence.

I love you. Your baby girl,

Tanya Rice

Introduction

As a young elementary school girl, I can recall growing up in the boondocks of Rockford, Illinois watching my mother and father leave the house late in the evening, leaving me and my siblings at home. My mother flaunted her spotless white dress as she embraced a little thick white book with a gold star on it. My father, a proud man sporting a black suit with an apron and briefcase in his hand. The first time I saw that apron, I thought he was getting ready to cook dinner. And contrary to popular belief, my father is a pretty good cook.

I was the epitome of a bookworm back then; therefore, I was enticed by *that white book*. For years, I begged my mother to read it, but she refused. I couldn't understand why someone who constantly stressed the importance of a good education would deny me the right to read it.

A sense of inquisitiveness and curiosity overtook my ability to obey my mother, so whenever she left the house, I would oftentimes find myself rummaging through her belongings trying to find *that white book*.

I often questioned her about *that white book,* her white dress, and my father's apron but as you might've guessed, she turned Madea on me and told me to "stay in a child's place." If you were reared by a Black Mother back in the day when Black Mothers were Black Mothers, I'm sure you can relate to that infamous phrase.

Order In The Order

As I got a little older, she began to take me to programs and events that her organization held. Before long, I came to realize that my mother was an active member of Princess Zorah Chapter #20 Order of the Eastern Star, and my father was a Prince Hall Mason hailing from Welcome Star Lodge #36 in Rockford, Illinois. That didn't explain much but, at least, I was making some progress. By the age of seven, I expressed interest in becoming an Eastern Star, but quite naturally; she told me that I wasn't old enough and I had to be at least eighteen years old (hold that thought).

I couldn't wait to turn 18. On my 18th birthday, I excitedly told my mother, "Momma, I'm 18, now I can become an Eastern Star!" Unfortunately, she told me they'd raised the minimum age to 21. My heart was crushed, but I knew that 21 was down the street and around the corner. In the meantime, I was STILL searching high and low-- trying to find *that white book* to no avail.

Fast forward to three years later, I messed around and turned 21. Once again, I excitedly told my mother, "Momma, I'm 21, now I can become an Eastern Star!" Ironically, they raised the age to 25, so I said to myself, "Hell no, something ain't right, momma is tripping!"

I asked my father if I could join and, of course, he told me to ask my mother. I asked my mother's Worthy Matron, her best friend whom I had known all my life, and she also told me to ask my mother. Unfortunately, my mother went home to be with the Lord before my 25th birthday. You will not believe that after her death, I went into overdrive trying to find *that white book* that I had been searching for years to no avail. I said Lord have mercy, momma must have taken *that white book* to the kingdom with her!

The day after my mother passed away, her Worthy Matron came to our house, and I asked her if I could join now (even though I wasn't 25 yet). She boldly told me that my mother didn't want me to join because I asked too many questions. Sadly, she was right, so all I could do was shake my head and walk away.

Despite being blackballed by my own mother, I never lost interest in becoming an Eastern Star. Three years later, I was getting ready to get off work one day at the post office in Atlanta Georgia when a mail carrier angrily returned from her route. She shouted, "Oh shit, I lost my husband's Masonic pen. He is going to kill me!" I was not the least bit concerned about her husband killing her, I immediately asked her if she was an Eastern Star. As she fumbled through her belongings, she said yes. I said to myself, Thank you JESUS! I told her I had been wanting to be one my whole life.

Long story short, I became a member of the Order of the Eastern Star on Tuesday, July 15, 1997, in College Park, Georgia. As I thumbed through the pages of *that white book* that was presented to me as a Ritual, I came across page 19 that stated the minimum requirements, the first thing that I noticed was that you must be at least **18** years of age. I laughed and said to myself, "Wow, Momma played me!"

Twenty-six years later, I am a proud Past Worthy Matron and founder of two Chapters in Houston, Texas. As I do the works of the Order, I feel my mother's presence hovering over me even though she blackballed me. She is my inspiration and my motivation. If AT&T had a tower in Heaven, I'd call and tell her that I FINALLY reached the minimum age to join the Order of The Eastern Star (which would probably be 75 if she was still alive) and that I'm doing my best to perform whatever duties that may devolve upon me.

Now that we have covered my journey into the Order, please accept my invitation to the study session. Before we begin, I feel compelled to ask, Are you a member of the Order of The Eastern Star? If your answer is yes or no, please close this informative book and return it to the sender. If you answered correctly, please grab your Ritual, Bible, highlighter, notepad, pen and any other supplies/materials you deem necessary, come inside room 357, and govern yourselves accordingly.

CHAPTER 1

Historical Sketch

On June 10, 1774, the Grand Orient of France established a new rite called, the Rite of Adoption. This was where the idea that the Master of the Lodge should be the Presiding Officer was adopted.

The Grand Orient is what we refer to today as the Grand Lodge while the Grand East is the seat of the Grand Master in the Grand Lodge. Adoptive Masonry originated in France but later spread throughout Europe. The Quadruple Lodge of the Nine Sisters was one of the most prominent Lodges.

In 1775 the Duchess of Bourbon was appointed as the Grand Mistress of Adoptive Masonry. Over 1,000 people from the elite French society were in attendance for her conferment. The Duchess of Bourbon was the wife of the Grand Master of the Grand Orient of France. In May 1775, she became the first person to receive the title of Grand Mistress. Grand Mistresses were highly esteemed ladies holding titles, such as Duchess, Empresses, Madame, and Princesses.

Their ceremonies were borrowed from the Carbonari or Coal burners. At this point, I am sure you are scratching your head wondering who the Carbonari or Coal burners were, right? In a nutshell, they were a group of Italian college students who wanted to overthrow the government, they felt that the government had too much control over their lives.

In 1801 Adoptive Masonry was established in Holland. It was dissolved on June 10, 1810 for unknown reasons. In 1805, Empress Josephine was installed as Grand Mistress of the Imperial Lodge of Adoption of French Chevaliers at Strasbourg. According to M. Boubee, the Father of French Masonry, this was the biggest event in the history of Adoptive Masonry.

The Adoptive Rite consisted of four degrees, Apprentice, Companion, Mistress and Perfect Mistress.

1. The Apprentice Degree was symbolic and introductory. It was used to improve the mind.

2. The Companion Degree depicted the scene of Temptation in the Garden of Eden. Candidates were reminded of the penalty incurred for such falls.

3. The Mistress Degree represented the Tower of Babel; Confusion of the tongue was a symbol of a badly regulated Lodge. While Jacobs Ladder was introduced as a moral lesson of Order and Harmony. It represented the alliance between Heaven and Earth. To this degree, the Mistress climbed the invisible ladder that led to perfection. Her foot was placed upon God's footstool (earth), while the summit rested on the throne of the Creator.

4. The Perfect Mistress degree represented Moses and Aaron, their wives, and the sons of Aaron. Moses and Aaron were the heads of the Israelites when the Egyptian army

was submerged in the Red Sea. This degree teaches us that we should never neglect our duty. It also symbolized the passage of humanity from a world of change and discord to a pure land of peace and rest.

The Officers of the Lodge of Adoption consisted of the Grand Master, Grand Mistress, Orator, Inspector, Inspectress, Depositor, Depositrix, Conductor and Conductress.

The room was divided into four sections, North, South, East and West. These four cardinal points represented the four corners of the earth. It signified that all humans are equally the work of the Creator of the universe wherever they are.

1. North - North America (Apprentice)

2. South - Africa (Companion)

3. East - Asia (Mistress/Master)

4. West - Europe (Perfect Mistress)

The business of the Lodge was conducted by the sisters, the brothers were there as assistants only.

In 1850 the Adoptive Rite was introduced in the United States by Dr Robert Morris. The Adoptive Rite consisted of The Eastern Star, Queen of the South and Amaranth. According to page 9 of the Ritual, Dr Morris got the ideas for formulating the degrees from the French Grand Orient.

CHAPTER 2

Dr Robert Morris

If you're still in room 357, that means I didn't bore you to death with that introduction. Let's dive into something a little more familiar to us. I hope that by now, you're familiar with Dr Robert Morris, the founder of the Eastern Star, if not, let me enlighten you.

Dr. Robert Morris was a lawyer, poet, educator, and lecturer. He was born Robert Williams Peckham on Aug 31, 1818, at 26 Rector St, New York, NY. He was the son of Robert Peckham and Charlotte Shaw. There are conflicting accounts of his birthplace, but evidence proves that he was born in New York. His parents were married in Taunton MA in 1811 and moved to NY in 1815. Both of his parents were teachers. When his parents separated in 1821, he and his brother John stayed with their father until he died in 1825, after which they moved to Massachusetts to live with their mother.

Their paternal grandmother fought for custody of him and his brother because they were the only male heirs. The court awarded his mother custody and they stayed with her until her death a few years later. Shortly after his mother's death, he went to live with his foster father John Morris until 1837. During this time, he changed his name to Robert Williams Morris. He received degrees in law and philosophy.

After he left the Morris family, he traveled south to Missouri, Kentucky, Tennessee, and Mississippi.

He met Charlotte Mendenhall in Shelby County Tennessee. Rumor has it that she was the daughter of one of the most prominent families in Mississippi. They married on May 26, 1841, and had nine children together.

On Mar 5, 1846, Dr Morris received Masonic Light in Oxford Mississippi in Oxford Lodge #33. He became a Master Mason on July 3, 1846, and a Heroine of Jericho in 1847.

Dr Morris became a teacher and President of Mount Sylvan Academy in Oxford Mississippi. Holmes County Masons hired him to become the Principal of Eureka Masonic College AKA the Little Red Schoolhouse in Richland Mississippi, 50 miles North of Jackson Mississippi.

The Little Red Schoolhouse operated from 1847-1861. It was established by several Masonic Lodges of Holmes County Mississippi who raised $3,400 to build it. Its original name was Richland Literary Institute. A cornerstone was laid there in 1847 but it was forced to close its doors because of the Civil War.

During the war, it was the home of Company C, 15th Mississippi Infantry Regiment AKA Quitman Rifles. After the Civil War, Holmes County used the abandoned school as a segregated public school for African Americans until the 1958-59 school year. In 1959 the Grand Chapter of Mississippi purchased it and it is now a shrine in honor of Dr. Robert Morris.

The Little Red Schoolhouse is the birthplace of the Eastern Star. Dr Morris conceived the ideas of the Eastern Star, wrote the first Ritual in 1849-1850, and conferred honorary degrees there. He also taught at the Masonic University in LaGrange Kentucky.

In Feb 1850, after a sharp attack of rheumatism, Dr Morris worked diligently on the formation of the organization. He gave his first lecture in Nov 1850 in Collierville Tennessee. His wife Charlotte, his Masonic brothers, and their wives were the first to receive the degree. This was the beginning of the Constellation period.

CHAPTER 3

Constellation Period

During the Constellation period, the Cabalistic Motto FATAL was Fairest among *Ten* Thousand *and* altogether lovely. In Song of Solomon chapter 5, that Motto represented Christ. Manuals were used instead of the Rituals we use today. The first Manual was called the Mosaic Book. The First Constellation recorded was Purity Constellation #2.

The five Heroines that we know today were Correspondents named after goddesses.

Adah was Luna (Roman) Goddess of the moon. Ruth was Flora (Roman) Goddess of flowers. Esther was Hebe (Greek) Goddess of Youth. She was the daughter of Zeus. She was the cupbearer for the gods/goddesses of Mount Olympus until she married Hercules. Hercules became the guardian/protector of the gates of Olympus. Martha was Thetis or Thesis (Greek) sea goddess. Electa ironically was Areme an Egyptian goddess.

In 1855, Morris formed the Supreme Constellation of the Eastern Star. Officers were called Luminaries. He was the Most Enlightened Grand Luminary. Their Headquarters was in New York. He issued over 100 charters throughout the US. The Constellation system was discontinued in 1860.

CHAPTER 4

Family System

The Family System replaced the Constellation System in 1860. The first Family System, Miriam Family #111 was formed in Illinois in 1866. Names of the goddesses were changed to biblical names; Adah, Ruth, Esther, Martha, and Electa as we know them today. Families were very similar to the Constellations.

The Cabalistic Motto was changed to FATAL. The Manual of the Eastern Star replaced the Mosaic Book. In 1865, the first Ritual, the Rosary of the Eastern Star was published, it was the last printed publication of the Family System. The Family System was discontinued in 1868.

In 1866, Dr Morris befriended another Mason named Robert Macoy of NY. In 1868, he transferred control of the organization to Macoy so that he could travel to the Holy Land. Morris formed the first Lodge in Jerusalem; Royal Solomon Mother Lodge #293 and was named the first Worshipful Master even though he never attended a meeting.

CHAPTER 5

Chapter System

In 1868, Robert Macoy introduced us to the Chapter System that we know today. The first Chapter, Alpha #1 was formed on Dec 28, 1868, in New York, NY. Robert Macoy's wife, Mrs. Eliza A. Macoy was the first candidate to become a member of the Order of the Eastern Star.

The first Grand Chapter was formed in Michigan on Oct 31, 1867. Today, the Order of the Eastern Star is the largest fraternal organization in the world to which men and women may belong. There are over 10,000 Chapters with over 1 million members.

The Eastern Star is divided into three eras:

I.   1850-1868 under the leadership of Dr Robert Morris.

II. 1868-1876 Rob Macoy - Chapter/Grand Chapter was formed.

III.1876 - present General Grand Chapter was founded by Willis Engle of Indiana.

By now, I'm sure you've noticed that in some instances, I referred to the Order of the

Eastern Star as the Eastern Star. That was intentional and please allow me to explain the reasoning.

CHAPTER 6

Rite vs Order

A Rite is an organized group of steps. The Adoptive Rite consisted of three steps: the Eastern Star, Queen of the South, and Amaranth.

An Order is a Rite of one or more degrees. There are five degrees in the Order of the Eastern Star: Adah, Ruth, Esther, Martha, and Electa.

An Order has a form of government with elected officers and by-laws. Neither the Constellation System nor the Family System had elected officers, Morris was a one-man show with no structure. The first Grand Chapter was formed in Michigan in 1867. It opened as a Grand Lodge of Adoption and closed as a Grand Chapter of the Order of The Eastern Star.

<u>Please take note that we, as members of the Order of the Eastern Star do NOT attend Lodge meetings nor are we members of ANY Lodge or Grand Lodge. We do not have a Grand Master, we have a Grand Patron. We attend Chapter meetings, not Lodge meetings, though some Chapters meet at a Lodge building. Though this is a fraternal organization, we are not a part of any fraternity or so-</u>

rority, so please don't get it twisted and stop the hazing!

On December 1, 1874, Queen Esther Chapter #1 in Washington DC became the first OES Chapter consisting of Black women. It was established by Brother Thornton A Jackson. He was their first Worthy Patron alongside their first Worthy Matron, Sister Martha Welch.

CHAPTER 7

Adah (daughter)

The Five Heroines whose virtues we strive to emulate each represent a phase in a woman's life: daughter, sister, wife, mother, and widow. I encourage you to read your Ritual and the respective Bible verses as we go into our Heroines. I won't regurgitate the whole story but rather expound on a few key points.

Our first heroine Adah is referred to as Jephthah's daughter in Judges Chapter 11. To understand Jephthah's daughter, I deem it necessary to introduce you to Jephthah himself.

After the days of Joshua and Moses, no central government existed. In times of crisis, the people were led by ad hoc leaders known as Judges.

ROLE OF JUDGES

1) A Judge was the highest governing official in the nation.

2) They acted as military leaders in times of trial.

3) They were chosen by God to rescue, rule and guide the Ancient Israelites.

4) Their functions were compared to that of a King, but they weren't anointed as kings.

5) They didn't make or interpret the laws. They administered God's Laws according to God's direction. To administer Laws according to God's direction, one must have contact with God himself.

6) Judges had to be invested with the Spirit of God, they were considered "holy men."

There was a total of 13 Judges. Othniel was the 1st Judge (Caleb's nephew).

Deborah was the 4th Judge, the first female Judge (1st woman to direct the affairs of a nation).

The Judge we're going to highlight today is the 9th Judge, Jephthah.

WHO IS JEPHTHAH?

He was a resident of Gilead (a rugged mountainous region East of the Jordan River situated in the Kingdom of Jordan) in the Bible the word means "hill of testimony" or "mound of witness."

He was the son of Gilead and a harlot AKA prostitute. After the death of his father, his brothers kicked him out of the house. They said he made the whole family look bad. They called him a reject and a "Child of Shame."

The Laws didn't protect the son of a harlot, so he was denied any of his father's inheritance. Because of his strained relationship with his brothers, he was forced to live in the Land of Tob with the thugs and rejects. Jephthah was a born leader, a mighty man of valor. He trained residents there to be soldiers. In essence, he was a modern-day gang leader. The Land of Tob is located east of Jordan, 13 miles southeast of the Sea of Galilee.

While living in Tob, the Elders of Gilead came to him and asked him to go to war with them against the Ammonites. (The Ammonites are the offspring of Lot and his youngest daughter; they were conceived through incest).

They promised to make him head of the Army of Israel. He asked them how they dared to come to him while in distress, reminding them that he was the same man who wasn't good enough to sleep in his father's house with his brothers. Eventually, he accepted their offer and went back to Gilead with them. He appeared with the Elders before the people and received their approbation.

Jephthah's selection as Leader and Judge was a 3 fold consideration:

1. He was selected by the Elders.

2. He was approved by the people.

3. He was sanctioned by God.

Before going to war, he tried to make peace with the King of the children of Ammon. The King was adamant about going to war saying the Israelites were occupying territory that rightfully belonged to Ammon. By this time the Israelites had been enslaved by the Egyptians, Amorites, Ammonites, Philistines, Amalekites, and the Moanites. Every time God delivered them from the oppression of the enemy, they'd worship a different God (Baalim being one). This practice is known as religious syncretism.

Jephthah knew how weak his army was and he was tired of losing so he made an irrevocable and unqualifiable vow unto the Lord. (Judges 11:30-31) "Lord, if thou shall without fail deliver the children of Ammon into mine hands, then it shall be that whatsoever cometh forth of the doors of my house to meet me when I return from the children of Ammon, shall surely be the Lord's and I will offer it up for a burnt offering." There were two types of human sacrifice; burnt offering and offer to the service of the Tabernacle.

The Lord answered his prayer and delivered the Ammonites into his hands. Their forces drove the enemy out of 20 cities and out of the huge plain of the vineyards. Everyone in Gilead cheered as the army came home. Jephthah was walking with his chest stuck out and his head held high until he went home. His ONLY daughter met him at the door with trembles and dance.

When he saw her, he tore his clothes in anguish and cried out, (Judges 11:35) "***Alas my daughter***, thou hast brought me very low, and thou art one who trouble me. I have opened my mouth unto the Lord, and I cannot go back!" Levitical Law taught that breaking a vow not only meant the forfeit of one's life, but it made one look bad.

Adah had only one request-- that she may go to the mountains for two months to prepare for her death (bewail her virginity). She prayed and sought communion with God to gain his Divine Assistance in facing the ordeal of her life.

She bewailed her virginity for 2 reasons:

1. Every Jewish maiden wanted to be the mother of the Messiah.

2. After she was executed there would be no heir because she was the only child.

At the end of the two months, she met her brokenhearted father and a multitude of people at the mountainside, the FATAL spot where the altar was erected. She gave him a long kiss goodbye.

Biblically she's known as Jephthah's Daughter as our founder Dr Rob Morris gave her that name because Adah means "ornament" and he felt she was an ornament to her people. The name Adah is only found twice in the Bible.

1. Genesis 4:19 - Wife of Lamech (the father of polygamy). She was the mother of Tubal Cain (hero of Masonic Lore) which is possibly where Dr Morris got the name from because of the Masonic connection.

2. Genesis 36:2 – Wife of Esau. Esau was the furry red twin brother of Jacob and the son of Isaac.

Pass: Alas my daughter

Color: Blue; clear skies after all clouds have vanished. Also represents fidelity and loyalty.

Flower: Violet; It grows in shaded and natural surroundings and is associated with meekness and humility.

Emblem: Sword & Veil. Together they represent Right and Revelation. The sword represents the concept that the sword must be taken up in the defense of right and the performance of duty. The veil symbolizes revelation. In the book of Revelation, the throne of God was separated from the rest of the heavenly court by a veil. The lifted veil symbolizes God's Word and Will revealed to the individual.

Christ symbol: The Open Bible - Adah sacrificed her life to fulfill her father's vow. Christ sacrificed his life for our sins.

Jewel: Turquoise; represents her character traits; obedience and loyalty

Season: Spring; her life represented springtime or early womanhood of life itself.

Beatitude: "Blessed are the pure in heart for they shall see God" Matthew 5:8.

CHAPTER 8

Ruth (widow)

The book of Ruth can be found in the Old Testament. It is one of the most interesting stories in the whole realm of literature. When Benjamin Franklin was the Ambassador to the Court of France, he attended a gathering of the literati of Paris. He was asked for a reading, and he took a manuscript out of his pocket and read the entire book of Ruth. People praised it as one of the jewels of literature, unaware that it was from the Bible.

Ruth was a Moabite and a descendant of Lot. Lot was the nephew of Abraham. Abraham was known as the father of many nations. He was saved from destruction in Sodom, but his wife turned into a pillar of salt. (Gen 19:26) Lot believed in the God of Abraham and the promises He made to him. When Abraham set out to go to an unknown land (Canaan) in response to God's command, "Lot went with him. He was not persuaded to go, he went voluntarily!" He too left behind the security of his native land and went out not knowing whither he went. (Genesis 121-5)

Lot's two daughters got him drunk and had sex with him in fear of losing humanity.

(Genesis: 19:30) Unbeknownst to him, he impregnated his oldest daughter, she had a son named Moab. Moab became the father of the Moabites. His youngest daughter had a son named Ben-Ammin, he became the father of the Ammonites. As I previously stated in the story of Adah, Jephthah defeated the Ammonites after making a vow unto the Lord.

The Moabites adored Chamos as their national god, they also worshiped Ashtar as his consort. Because of their idolatry, the Moabites became an abomination unto God and stayed that way until Ruth met Boaz on the threshing floor in Bethlehem.

Bethlehem means House of Bread but ironically a famine in Bethlehem forced Elimelech, his wife Naomi, and their two sons; Mahlon and Chilion to move to Moab. They worshipped God faithfully. Chilion married Orpah while Mahlon married a Gentile named Ruth, the daughter of King Eglon.

King Eglon, the son of King Balak, reigned over the Israelites for 18 years. One day he was approached by Judge Ehud, a Benjamite who told him that he had a message for him from God. King Eglon dismissed his assistants and welcomed him in. Judge Ehud the 2nd Judge, stabbed him in his abdomen with a double-edged sword, locked the door then left. The King tried to remove the sword but the layers of fat on his stomach wouldn't allow him to. After impatiently waiting for what seemed like days, his assistants unlocked the door only to find King Eglon dead in a pile of feces. (Judges 3:19-22)

Within 10 years, Naomi's husband and both of her sons died. Naomi means sweetness but she became so bitter she changed her name. (Ruth 1:20) "Do not call me Naomi, call me Mara, for the Almighty has dealt very bitterly with me." Rumor has it that they were punished for not being faithful to God. On his deathbed, Mahlon instructed Ruth to go to Bethlehem with his mother Naomi because the people of God lived there.

Naomi heard that God visited the people of Bethlehem and left food, so she decided it was time to return home. She told Ruth and Orpah to go home to their family. Ruth clung to her. She asked the Lord to punish her if she left her mother-in-law. "Entreat me not to leave thee." (Ruth 1:16-17) She told Naomi that she'd stick with her until death did them part. Orpah, on the other hand, kissed Naomi farewell, chunked the deuces then left. Rumor has it that after Naomi departed, she slept with 100 men and a dog in one night. (Ruth Rabbah 2:20) The Philistine Goliath who fought the young David during the battle in the Valley of Elah was born of this promiscuous activity. (1 Samuel 17)

If you ever hear the phrase, "May the sons of the one who kissed come and fall by the hand of the sons of the one who clung." It is the story of David (Ruth) vs Goliath (Orpah). It has been alleged that Oprah Winfrey is named after Orpah, but people pronounce her name Oprah so that's what she answers to, allegedly her birth certificate reads Orpah Gail Winfrey.

Ruth and Naomi returned to Bethlehem poor as ever but determined to survive, luckily it was harvesting season, so Ruth went to glean in the fields. After a long day's work, she only had two handfuls of barley. People laughed and insulted her. She was tired, hungry, thirsty, and frustrated so she sat under a tree to rest.

While under the tree, Boaz the owner of the field noticed her and asked the foreman of the field, "Whose damsel is this?" (Ruth 2:5) Boaz told the men not to ridicule her but to help her out. He invited her to eat, drink, and glean with the other women.

At the end of the day, Ruth took so much barley home to Naomi that she asked her whose field she worked in. Ruth told her about a man named Boaz. Boaz was the richest man in Bethlehem, a wellknown and charitable man. He was the son of a harlot named Rahab and Salmon (Elimelech's brother). Naomi informed her that was her husband's relative.

The next day, Ruth went back to the field and Boaz gave her even more food and invited her to eat with them. Naomi told her to uncover his feet and lay there after he got full and drunk. She followed Naomi's instructions and laid at his feet all night long.

Boaz told her about her husband's next of kin. He gathered the elders of the city to witness their encounter. Boaz allowed him the opportunity to marry Ruth, but he said, Nah, I'm good. He gave Boaz his shoe and he and Ruth were united in holy matrimony. In Jewish custom, exchanging a shoe was like signing a contract.

Ruth and Boaz had a son named Obed. They allowed Naomi to raise him since she lost both of her sons. Now, if you will, let's exit room 357 for a minute and go to Ruth and Boaz's family reunion at Levings Lake Park. If you're not familiar with Levings Lake, use your GPS. On that note, don't forget to thank our Melanated sister, Dr Gladys West for her wonderful lifesaving and gas-saving invention because we would all be lost without it.

Y'all ready? Walk with me now.

While at the family reunion, I overheard Big Mama tell Aunt Gladys and Aunt B that Obed became the father of Jesse. Jesse was the father of King David. King David was the father of King Solomon (the wisest man who ever lived). King David had a brother named Shimea. Shimea had a son named Jair. Jair had a son named Mordecai. Jair had a brother named Abihail. Abihail had a daughter named Esther. This makes Esther and Mordecai cousins, he's clearly not her uncle as you may have heard. Ruth is King David's great-grandmother. David is Esther's great-uncle, which makes Ruth Esther's great great-great-aunt.

In direct lineage, we find that the Messiah was a descendant of Ruth. (Matthew 1:1-16) Shimea cursed David (1 Samuel 16:5). David told King Solomon to kill Shimea (1 Kings 2:8). Girl, these family reunions are a hot mess, aren't they? Sit next to Big Mama, Aunt B, and Aunt Gladys AKA the Big Three, and you will get the scoop on everything and everybody! I'm just saying. Now, if you will, kindly pour your drink out, and let's head back to room 357.

Pass: Who is this? (Genesis 2:5)

Color: Yellow; Sincere affection and that which is diving. Color of the rising sun. Ripened grain, thanking heaven for the privileges of furnishing daily bread.

Flower: Yellow Jasmine. Midsummer flower that best portrays the humble life of those who walk the paths of loneliness and virtue. It is a token of the patient industry, and its color is an emblem of plenty.

Emblem: Sheaf of Wheat which symbolizes the collective greatness of an accumulated succession of small deeds or duties.

Christ Symbol: Lily of the Valley. Meekness and humbleness. Ruth left her native land for the sake of her religion and her fellow man.

Jewel: Topaz. Humble and fulfillment of duty.

Season: Summer; summer of life with its abundance and growth. The fruitful harvest of life.

Beatitude: Blessed are the meek, for they shall inherit the earth (Matthew 5:5)

The story of Ruth teaches us that we might have to relinquish our most cherished things to be true friends.

CHAPTER 9

Esther (wife)

The Book of Esther was written between 492 BC and 460 BC. The author is unknown. The book of Esther can be found in the Old Testament between Nehemiah and Job. Esther was a Jewish damsel born in 500 BC. I know you're probably wondering how the Book of Esther was written between 492 BC and 460 BC, but she wasn't born until 500 BC right? Well, let me break it down for you, Aunt B and Aunt Gladys told me at the family reunion that the author was a psychic, and he predicted her life 40 years before she was born. Amazing right? Nope, let me straighten my crown, I forgot we left Levings Lake, so I need to get serious.

In the BCE (Before Common Era) also known as BC (Before Christ) each year decreased; it went from 2500 BC – 1BC. In 2500 the next year was 2499 BC, 2498 BC, etc. In the AD era (Anno Domini which means year of our Lord) also known as After Death, the numbers increased; last year was 2023, this year it's 2024 and next year will be 2025. AD is from 1 – infinity. Still confused, please call 605-477-3018 and I'll break it down in laymen's terms for you, operators are standing by.

Esther is one of two books in the Bible named after a woman, the other being Ruth. It is one of the most controversial books in the Bible because it doesn't mention God's name at all. Even though God's name is never mentioned his guiding hand can be seen throughout.

The story takes place in Susa (Capital of Persia). Susa is one of the oldest cities in the world. Daniel and Nehemiah both lived in Susa and Daniel's tomb is in that city. It is 250 miles East of Babylon, 75 miles East of the Tigris River, and 250 miles North of the Persian Gulf.

Esther is an old Persian word that means Star. Her birth name is Hadassah which is a Jewish name that means Myrtle. The Myrtle Tree was native to Babylonia, but Jewish exiles took it with them, and it became a symbol of Israel.

Hadassah was an orphan. Her mother and father Abihail died, so her cousin Mordecai became her guardian. During the third year of his reign, King Ahasuerus (Xerxes) decided it was time to celebrate. King Xerxes was Persia's 5th King, he ruled from 486 to 465 BC, and he was one of the wealthiest people in the world.

The King had a General Feast that lasted 180 days. Some scholars said he was trying to solicit military allegiance because he was getting ready to invade Greece. He invited everyone in all 127 provinces of Persia. Keep in mind that Persian territory stretched from India to Cush (modern-day Ethiopia), a total of 2678 miles.

After the General Feast, the King ordered a Splendid Feast that only lasted seven days. The Splendid Feast was the After Hour at the hole in the wall (LoL). This feast (AKA Grand Council) was held in the courtyard of the palace and only the elite people of royal lineage with wealth and influence were invited, Dukes, Lords, Princes, Nobles, Kings, etc. This was also a fundraiser to help him fund the war with Greece.

At the same time, the king's wife Queen Vashti was hosting a similar party for the women of Susa. Vashti means excellence and a beautiful woman. After the King got drunk, he decided he wanted to show off his beautiful wife, so he sent seven chamberlains/eunuchs to get her. ~~He told her to~~ ~~bring a ½ pint of Crown Royal.~~ LoL, I meant to say, he told her to appear wearing her royal crown. (Esther 1:11)

Queen Vashti knew her role, so she didn't go. It was a Jewish custom that when the kings got drunk, they called for their concubines, not their wives. This made the king furious, and he burned with anger. He felt she disobeyed and humiliated him. He called seven of his advisors to see what should be done to her. They advised him to dethrone her because if she got away with it all women would disobey their husbands.

As time went on, the king got lonely and felt he needed a new queen. He sent word that he wanted a "beautiful, young virgin." All the contestants lived in the house of women. Hegai was the chamberlain in charge.

Mordecai brought Hadassah a *fine white silk robe* and she entered the pageant. Her name was changed to Esther to hide her Jewish identity. Hegai immediately loved Esther, so he gave her the best place in the palace along with seven maidens.

All the contestants were prepared for 12 months, they were massaged with myrrh (used for anointing) for six months, then massaged with perfumes and oils to enhance their appearance for six months. The candidates for queenship became his concubines and were ordered to stay at the house until the king called on them. They were prohibited from getting married, having sex with other men, or leaving the house.

When Esther appeared before the king wearing her elegant white robe, he fell in love with her. He set the royal crown upon her head and declared her queen. Esther was the only candidate who worshiped a true God. She didn't worship idols or heathen gods.

She was in touch with divine power, and she won the world's first beauty pageant.

After Esther became the Queen, Mordecai became the gatekeeper of the courtyard. He walked by the palace daily to check on her. One day a fellow Jew named Barnabus told Mordecai that the king's eunuchs Bigthana and Teresh were plotting to kill him. Mordecai told Esther and after they investigated it, they were both sentenced to death and hung from a tree. It was recorded in the king's chronicles (public record) what Mordecai did.

Haman an Amalekite, the king's favorite was promoted to Prime Minister. The King decreed that everyone should bow to him and pay reverence. This was a form of civil respect. Everyone complied except Mordecai. Haman and Mordecai's beef dates to the times when Saul was King of Israel.

Haman, the son of Hammedatha the Amalekite hated Jews. The Amalekites attacked Israel when they came out of Egypt, so God told Saul through the prophet Samuel to attack the Amalekites and destroy everything that belonged to them: men, women, children, infants, cattle, sheep, donkeys, and camels. (1 Samuel 15) Saul attacked the Amalekites but spared the life of Agag their king.

Saul's disobedience caused discord between the Benjamites and Amalekites. Aside from the historical beef, Haman was jealous of Mordecai. After Haman felt Mordecai disrespected him, he wanted to kill him. When they assured him that Mordecai was a Jew, he wanted to kill all the Jews in the kingdom. They cast lots to determine which day they'd carry out their mission. The 13th day of the 12th month of Adar was the date set. Jewish people used two calendars: civil and sacred. Per the sacred calendar, Adar is the third month on our calendar.

Haman informed the king that there was a "certain group of people around our kingdom whose laws are different from ours, therefore they're breaking our laws and need to be dealt with." Haman was adamant about killing the Jews, so he offered to pay 10,000 talents of silver.

A talent is a unit of weight/currency in silver and gold. Because the value of silver and gold fluctuates, I'm going to use the conversion that I did in 2012. At that time, 1 talent was worth $1,200 therefore 10,000 x $1,200 = $12,000,000.00. I don't know about you, but I've seen people do more for less.

The deal was sealed, and the date was set for March 13th. An edict was sent throughout Persia that all Jews were to be killed on that day. When word got back to Mordecai, he tore his clothes in anguish and put on sackcloth with ashes then went out into the middle of the city and cried out to the Lord. Then he went to the gates of the king's palace to tell Esther. Sackcloth is made of black goat's hair, it's very coarse and is worn by mourners as an outward sign of mourning.

Mordecai sent a copy of the decree to Esther and advised her to go to the king so she could save her people from extirpation. Esther told Mordecai that she could be killed by going to the king without being summoned. He had not called on her for 30 days. Mordecai gave her a reality check and told her not to forget where she came from. He advised her not to get brand new and then reiterated to her that even though she was the Queen of Persia, she was still a Jew. He informed her that God planned to place her in that position to save her people at a time like this. Esther sent word to Mordecai to have all the Jews in Susa fast and pray for three days along with her maidens then she'd go before the king to make a request. "The effectual fervent prayer of a righteous man availeth much." (James 5:16)

What is Fasting?

Acts 13:2 and 14:23 record believers fasting before they make important decisions. Fasting and praying are often linked together according to Luke 2:37. Too often, the focus of fasting is on the lack of food.

Instead, the purpose of fasting should be to take your eyes off the things of this world to focus solely on God. Fasting is a way to demonstrate to God, and ourselves that we are serious about our relationship with Him. Fasting helps us gain a new perspective and renewed reliance upon God.

On the third day, as Esther walked past the Sentinel and gatekeepers, she sang a song that we sang in the young adult choir at Macedonia Baptist Church, "If I perish, let me perish, for I'm going to meet the King." When he saw her, he was furious, and in the back of his mind he was thinking, "Doesn't she know what happened to Queen Vashti!" When she went before him, she gave him a sign and he held out his golden scepter and said, "**What wilt thou,** Queen Esther? And what is thy request? It shall be given to thee up to the half of the kingdom."

A scepter is a rod held by a ruler in a Monarch as a symbol of authority. Holding out a scepter means you have gained favor with the king. A touch from the king changes everything.

Esther requested a banquet with the king and Haman. Haman was so overjoyed he went home and bragged to his wife Zeresh and his friends. They told him that now was the perfect time to kill Mordecai. They told him to prepare a gallows 50 cubits high to hang Mordecai. A gallows is a wooden frame used for lynching. I'm mathematically inquisitive so I did the math to see how high 50 cubits were. To start with, 1 cubit = 18 inches. 50 x 18 = 900 inches. There are 12 inches in a foot so 900/12 = 75 feet.

After the banquet, the King was restless, so he read the chronicles and realized that Mordecai saved his life when his two gatekeepers plotted to kill him. He felt obligated to reward Mordecai. Fate was on Esther's side and Haman's plan was about to backfire on him.

The next day at the second banquet, the King asked Esther again, "What is thy petition? It shall be given to you up to the half of the kingdom." Esther told him that Haman was plotting to kill her and her fellow Jews. The King was furious at Haman and ordered that he be hung on the gallows that he prepared for Mordecai. After Haman's death, the King gave Esther his estate and she let Mordecai rule over it.

Mordecai wrote a decree reversing the extirpation of the Jews but advised them to stand back and stand by. On the 13th day of Adar (Mar 13), the Jews killed 500 men in Susa as well as Haman's 10 sons. Throughout the 127 provinces, 75,000 people were killed by the stroke of a mighty sword. The next day they celebrated a day that turned from sorrow to joy. That day is called the Feast of Purim. Mordecai wrote that Jews should celebrate that day yearly and they still do it today. In 2024, it was celebrated on March 23 - 24.

After it was all said and done, Esther sang a song called, No Weapon Formed against Me Shall Prosper. If you'd like to hear her beautiful rendition, press the page # in the bottom right corner and hold it for five seconds.

Pass: What wilt thou?

Color: White; represents purity and innocence. Keep your robe white and unspotted from the ruins of the world.

Flower: White lily, a symbol of purity and peace. A lily is pure and spotless.

Emblem: Crown and Scepter. A crown represents the highest honors. The scepter represents power. A crown and scepter united represent forces of power and authority welded together to ensure justice for all.

Christ Symbol: Sun. The sun is the source of light, strength, and power. Esther's enlightened leadership made her the strength and power of the Jews. Christ is the son of righteousness and the enlightenment of the world. He is the source of power and strength for all men.

Jewel: Diamond. Her character was flawless, and her life was very valuable to her people.

Beatitude: Blessed are the peacemakers for they shall be called the children of God. (Matthew 5:9)

CHAPTER 10

Martha (sister)

The story of Martha can be found in John 11 and Luke 10:38-42. Martha is the first Heroine whose story is in the New Testament. She was born in Judah Province, modern-day Israel. Her family consisted of herself, her brother Lazarus, and her sister Mary. Martha's family were faithful followers of Christ.

She was more aggressive and outgoing than her sister Mary. She was born in a royal lineage; her father Syro was the Duke of Syria.

Martha and her siblings lived in Bethany, a town 1 ½ miles from Jerusalem near Mount Olives and North of Jericho. They lived in a castle. Martha and her family were close personal friends of Jesus.

Jesus said in Matthew 8:20, "Foxes have holes and birds of the air have nests, but I, the Son of Man have no place to lay his head." Jesus had a home in Bethany, the household of Martha, Mary, and Lazarus.

When Jesus was away, Lazarus got sick and died. He had been dead for four days by the time Jesus returned. When Martha heard he was coming across the mountains, she ran to him, fell on her knees, and said, "Lord, if thou hadst been here, my brother had not died. But I know that even now, whatsoever thou wilt ask of God he will give it to thee. (John 11:21)

While on her knees, Martha gave a sign of a perfect triangle; the holy trinity which represents God the Father, the one who rules, God the Son, the creator of all things and God the Holy Ghost, the completer of all material things. The shortest scripture in the Bible John 11:35 occurred in this scene, which says, "Jesus wept."

After four days the body becomes decomposed and has a bad odor. However, Jesus called his name and Lazarus rose from the dead four days later with his grave clothes on and walked like a new man.

Around 48 AD, after the death of Jesus, Martha left Judah and went to Provence (Southeast France) and started converting people to the Christian faith. Lazarus had to flee Judah because of plots on his life. He became the first Bishop of Kiton, Cyprus. Cyprus is an island east of the Mediterranean Sea, east of Greece, south of Turkey, west of Syria, and north of Egypt. He was appointed bishop by Paul and Barnabas. He lived there for 30 years and was buried for the second and final time there.

Martha moved to Tarascon, France. Tarascon was named after the dragon Tarasque which killed three hundred men daily. The dragon was half beast, half fish, and was said to be stronger than twelve lions. This dragon was drowned ships and if you touched it you burned.

People knew that Martha was close friends with Jesus and was filled with the Holy Ghost, so they asked her to contain the dragon. Martha fasted and prayed daily. She only ate once a day and prayed 100 times during the day and 100 times during the night.

She went into the woods and saw the dragon eating a man. She poured holy water on it and showed him a cross. The dragon stood still as a sheep as she bound him with her girdle, and everyone stuck spears and glaives in him. A girdle was magical, it gave power, strength, and protection. A glaive is a single edge blade on the end of a pole. Since 1474 there has been an annual celebration in Tarascon for Martha defeating the folkloric creature. Before her death in Tarascon, Martha converted many people to Christianity.

Martha's pass: Believeth Thou This (John 11:26) this pass was given by Jesus.

Color: Green; a symbol of eternity.

Flower: Fern - represents eternal life. Faith in the immortality of the soul.

Emblem: Broken Column which represents life cut off in the vigor of manhood.

Christ Symbol: Lamb and Cross.

Beatitude: Blessed are they that mourn for they shall be comforted. (Matt 5:4)

CHAPTER 11

Electa (mother)

In the early days of Christianity, the ruling authorities feared the Christians would rebel and make them lose their power. This made the political environment tense and chaotic. To coerce them to renounce their Christian faith, the Romans threatened Christians with abuse, imprisonment, and death.

At the age of ninety, St John the Evangelist was one of the Christian church's most revered and recognized authorities. In 2 John, he wrote a heartfelt letter to The Elect Lady and her children warning them to beware of false prophets and not to be guilty of associating with them. He commended her for obeying the commandments and advised her that one must love God before obeying them. He advised her to love her friends and enemies.

Electa, the Ideal Mother, was an educated lady of high repute and strong convictions. According to today's standards, she ran a homeless shelter in her mansion. She was known around the country of Judah for her philanthropy and benevolence.

Roman soldiers went to Electa's home demanding that she renounce her Christian faith but she refused. She and her entire family were dragged to prison for one year. After serving one year in prison, she was given another opportunity, but she refused. This time she and her entire family were crucified. She became a source of strength to many Christians throughout the years. As she was about to expire, Electa said, "Forgive them Father for they know not what they do!"

Electa's Pass: Love One Another.

Color: Red; Love and hospitality.

Flower: The Red Rose; Represents her love for God, her family, and her fellow man.

Emblem: Cup; Represents one's allotted portion of life's joy and sorrows.

Christ Symbol: Lion; Symbol of power and strength.

Beatitude: Blessed are those who are persecuted for righteous sake for theirs is the kingdom of heaven. (Matthew 5:10)

CHAPTER 12

Landmarks (page 13)

1. The Eastern Star is the basis of the **five degrees** of the Adoptive Rite, the names and characters of the Rite are unchangeable.

Five degrees; Adah, Ruth, Esther, Martha, and Electa

2. Its lessons are **scriptural**, its teachings are **moral, and** its **purposes** are beneficent.

Its lessons are scriptural:

Adah - Judges 11:29-40

Ruth - Book of Ruth

Esther - Book of Esther

Martha - John 11

Electa - 2 John

Its teachings are **moral:**

Adah - integrity (fidelity)

Ruth - loyalty (constancy)

Esther - justice (loyalty)

Martha - faithfulness (faith)

Electa - love

Its **purposes** are beneficent:

Purposes: comfort, protect, and aid each other in our journey through the Labyrinth of human life.

__Beneficent__ = Performing acts of kindness and charity.

3. Its *__obligations__* are based on the honor of the female sex who obtain its ceremonies and are framed upon the principle that whatever benefits are due by the Masonic Fraternity to their wives, widows, daughters, and sisters of Masons, corresponding benefits are due from them to the brotherhood.

__Obligations__ page 93 & page 125 in your Ritual. Secrecy, obedience to laws, advice, sympathy, and aid. You are obligated to be your brother's keeper as well as your sister's keeper. Scratch my back and I'll scratch yours!

4. Each candidate shall declare a belief in the existence of a *__Supreme Being__*, who will sooner or later punish the willful violation of a solemn pledge.

__Supreme Being__ = Higher authority; God, Yahweh, Allah, Jehovah, etc. No special mention of religious belief or preference. However, you <u>cannot</u> be an atheist.

If you violate your obligation made to God (not the Chapter or the Order) willfully you will be punished sooner or later. Per Jewish custom, if you went against your word your name was scandalized or you were put to death. Remember Jephthah in Judges 11:35?

In God's law, a vow was a promise to God that should not be broken. It carries as much weight as a contract. (Numbers 30:1 and Deuteronomy 23:21-23)

5. The ***modes of recognition*** which are peculiar secrets of the Rite, cannot, without destroying the foundation of the system be changed.

Modes of recognition - signs, pass, and grip (page 126)

6. A ***covenant*** of secrecy voluntarily assumed is ***perpetual***: from the force of such obligation, there is no possibility of release.

Covenant - An agreement or promise between two or more parties. (Genesis 9:9 and 17:2) Perpetual - Never ending or changing.

Once you make a promise or take an oath of obligation there is no turning back. Even if you become an inactive member of the Order, you are still obligated to live by and remember your oath of obligation. Never talk OES to nonmembers. On that note, I highly recommend each of you to read the Covenant of Adoption on page 93 daily and live by it.

7. The control of the Rite lies in the State Grand Chapter of the Adoptive Rite.

As members of a subordinate Chapter, we are governed by the Constitution and By-laws of your Grand Chapter. Per white Ritual, the wording may vary if you have a gray Ritual.

8. The ballot for Candidates for membership must be ***unanimous*** and is to be kept inviolably ***secret.***

Unanimous – everyone must agree. One black ball rejects a Candidate.

Secret – Do not disclose to anyone how you voted – take it to the grave with you.

9. It is the right of every Chapter to be the judge of who shall be admitted into its membership and to select its own officers, but in no case can the ceremonies of the Order be conferred unless a Master Mason in good standing in the Masonic Fraternity presides.

Per Landmark #8, each Chapter has the right to ballot on its Candidates. The ballot box is equivalent to a weed eater used to keep unwanted weeds out of your garden.

Every Chapter is required to elect their officers annually and the Worthy Matron appoints the others.

A Master Mason presides over initiations and conferring of degrees. (Page 67)

10. Every member is amenable to the laws and regulations of the Order and may be tried for offenses, though he or she may permanently or temporarily reside in the jurisdiction of another Chapter.

Example: If you commit a crime and then move to another jurisdiction, you can still be tried for the offense.

11. It is the right of every member to appeal from the decision of a Subordinate Chapter to the Grand Chapter of the State.

I don't want to touch on this subject, but my advice is to follow your chain of command and let the Grand Chapter be your last resort.

12. It is the prerogative of the ***Grand Patron*** to preside over every assembly of the Rite wherever he may visit and to grant Dispensation for the formation of new Chapters within the ***state***.

The Grand ***Patron*** of your Grand ***Chapter*** can visit any Chapter within his jurisdiction.

If he enters the Chapter while it's in session, the alarm at the door is announced, the Worthy Matron gives three gavel raps, the Chapter rises and gives the Grand Honors sign, and the Conductress (or Marshal) escorts him to the East. (This may vary per jurisdiction) Dispensation – System of rules for governing affairs, official exemption from a law or obligation.

13. Every Chapter has the right to dispense the Light of the Adoptive Right and to administer its own private affairs.

There is no mandated syllabus or protocol on what, when, and how to teach/learn about the Order. Each Chapter can do so accordingly.

14. Every Chapter should elect and install its officers annually.

Per page 183, The Worthy Patron presides over elections which are to be held annually before the Festival of St John the Evangelist on Dec 27.

15. Every member may visit and sit in every regular Chapter, except when such a visitor is likely to disturb the harmony or interrupt the progress of the Chapter he or she proposes to visit.

As a financial member of the Order, you're entitled to visit another Chapter pending approval of the Worthy Matron unless a member of that Chapter objects in writing. You must have a current dues card and be prepared to pass a Recognition Test before entrance.

This too may vary per jurisdiction/affiliation

CHAPTER 13

Beatitudes

What are Beatitudes?

Beatitudes are a Set of teachings by Jesus in the Sermon on the Mount. Beatitude comes from the Latin word "beatus " which means happy, fortunate, or blissful. There are a total of eight Beatitudes.

Beatitudes focus on Love and Humility. (Humility

- Quality of being humble)

Each Beatitude Contains two phrases: Condition and the Result

Example: Condition - Blessed are the peacemakers

Result - for they shall be called the children of God

- It was Jesus' Longest recorded Sermon; it lasted several days.

-It took place early in Jesus' ministry after he was baptized by John the Baptist.

- It was a sermon given on the hillside by Capernaum.

"Blessed" describes a feeling of inner joy and peace you feel when you're right with Jesus.

HEROINES BEATITUDES

ADAH: Sixth Beatitude

Matthew 5:8; Blessed are the pure in heart, for they shall see God.

PURE - Cleansed from within; made clean and holy.

RUTH: Third Beatitude

Matt 5:5; Blessed are the MEEK, for they shall inherit the earth.

MEEK - Those who submit to God's authority; God's children will inherit everything. This scripture was highly praised by Mahatma Gandhi.

ESTHER: Seventh Beatitude

Matt 5:9; Blessed are the peacemakers for they will be called the children of God

PEACEMAKERS: Not only live in peace with others but promote peace within God and Man. MARTHA: Second Beatitude

Matt 5:4; Blessed are they that mourn for they shall be comforted.

MOURN: Feel or show deep sorrow or regret for some or their death.

ELECTA: Eighth Beatitude

Matt 5:10;_Blessed are they which are persecuted for righteous sake, for theirs is the kingdom of Heaven.

CHAPTER 14

Brain Teaser Tuesday

1. The Five Degrees of the Order of the Eastern Star are founded on the ___ _____.

2. Whose badge of office are the crossed pens within the Star?

3. Whose duty is it to guard and protect the interests of the Chapter?

4. Who makes the first impression upon a Candidate?

5. Whose emblem is the Baton within the Star?

6. What do two blows of the gavel do?

7. What do the five distinct raps at the door represent?

8. Who invites the Worthy Matron and other officers into the Chapter room?

9. When can a member's Badge be reversed?

10. Whose jewel is the Crossed Batons within a Star?

11. According to the Ritual, there are **three** places where a burial ceremony can be

held, what are they?

12. According to the Ritual, which two officers can be compensated if approved before elections?

13. What is the Special Motto?

14. Which flag takes precedence over all others?

15. Which heroine said, "Lord if thou hadst been here, my brother had not died?" Who was her brother?

16. Which Heroine went to jail and for how long?

17. The illustration below is the first page in your Ritual. It's very enlightening and filled with symbolism. Identify each sign and/or symbol in each section. There's a total of 14. Have fun!

1. Whose Emblem was changed? What was it originally and what is it now?

2. Where was Jephthah when asked to be the leader of the army?

3. What three places can a Burial Service be held?

4. Which three Heroines make up the Triangle of Battle? Why were they chosen?

5. Who painted the first OES Signet?

6. What is Mount Sylvan Academy??? Where is it located???

7. When and where was the first Eastern Star Chapter formed? What was the name of it?

8. What is the proper way to sit in the Chapter room?

9. Is it proper to sit with your legs crossed?

10. I am an elevated stone or tablet on which sacrifices were offered, what am I?

11. When the Bible is open on the Altar, it creates a Holy area between the prepared _____ and the _____, and no one is permitted to pass between these two places.

12. While she was expiring and about to pass to a better land, she prayed with her dying breath: Father, forgive them, for they know not what they do! Who is she?

13. I am from Moab. I am a descendant of Lot. Who am I?

14. What did Naomi say to call her and why?

15. Match the Central Division of the Star with the Heroine:

    Refulgent Sun-

    Lily of the Valley-

Lamb and a Cross-

Lion- Open Bible-

16. Match the flower with the heroine.

Violet-

White Lily-

Red Rose-

Yellow Jasmine-

The Fern-

17. I am known as the Lady of High Repute in the land of Judea. I was born to a noble family. Who am I?

HISTORICAL SKETCH TEST

1. What year was the Rite of Adoption Established?

2. Who established it?

3. What is the Grand Orient?

4. What is the Grand East?

5. What year was Adoptive Masonry established in France?

6. What year was Adoptive Masonry established in Holland?

7. When was it dissolved?

8. How many degrees did it consist of?

9. Name the degrees and explain each one.

10. What did the fourth degree symbolize?

11. Name the Nine officers of the Lodge of Adoption.

12. The room was divided into four sections, what did they represent?

13. For whom were the two thrones erected in the East?

14. Who is the Father of French Masonry?

15. What did he say was the biggest event in Adoptive Masonry?

16. The ceremonies of the Lodge were borrowed from whom?

17. What year was the Adoptive Rite introduced in the US?

18. Where did they borrow the idea of formulating the degrees?

ROBERT MORRIS TEST

1} What was Robert Morris' birth name?

2} When & Where was Robert Morris born?

3} Where did he get the last name Morris?

4} When & where did he receive Masonic Light?

5} When did he become a Master Mason?

6} When did he become a Heroine of Jericho?

7} Who hired him to become the Principal of Eureka Masonic College?

8} Where is Eureka Masonic College? What is it also known as?

9} What is the birthplace of The Eastern Star?

10} When and where did Robert Morris give his first lecture?

11} What were the Heroines called during the Constellation Period?

12} What was the Cabalistic Motto called during that period?

13} Who was Electa during the Constellation Period?

14} What was the name of the first Constellation?

15} What year was the Supreme Constellation of the Eastern Star formed?

16} What year was the Constellation Period discontinued?

17} What was the second period called?

18} What was the name of the first Family? What state were they from? What year were they founded?

19} What were the Correspondent's names changed to?

20} What was the Cabalistic Motto changed to?

21} What year was the first Ritual printed? What was it called?

22} What year was the Family Period discontinued?

23} Who did Dr Robert Morris transfer control to? What year?

24} Where did Dr Morris travel to?

25} What did he do while he was there?

26} What system was formed after The Family Period?

27} What was the name of the first Chapter? When and where was it formed? Who was the first OES Candidate?

28} What's the difference between a Rite and an Order?

29} The Eastern Star is divided into three eras, what are they?

30} What was the first Black Chapter? When and where was it started? Who was the first Black WM and WP?

31} What opened as a Grand Lodge of Adoption and closed as a Grand Chapter of the Order of the Eastern Star?

Bonus Question

Why do you think Dr Morris' first two systems were unsuccessful?

ADAH TEST

1. How many times is the name "Adah" mentioned in the scripture?

2. What does Adah mean?

3. Where does the story take place?

4. What is Adah's emblem(s)?

5. Who is Jephthah?

6. How many years did he serve as Judge?

7. Name two roles of a Judge.

8. How many Judges were there? What # Judge was Jephthah?

9. Who was the first Judge?

10. Who was the first female Judge? What # was she?

11. Who were Jephthah's parents?

12. Why did his brothers kick him out of the house?

13. Why didn't his father try to stop them?

14. Where was Jephthah's home?

15. Where was he when the elders came to him?

16. Jephthah's selection as Leader and Judge was a 3-fold consideration. What was the process?

17. What is Adah's pass?

18. Why was it given to her? By whom was it given?

19. What vow did Jephthah make to the Lord?

20. How many brothers and sisters did Adah have?

21. Why did Adah bewail her virginity?

22. How long did Adah stay in the mountains?

23. Together the sword and veil represent what?

24. In the book of Revelation, the throne of God was separated from the rest of the heavenly court by what?

25. What is the Christ symbol of this degree?

26. What season does Adah represent?

27. What is her beatitude?

28. In what scripture can you find the story of Jephthah's Daughter?

VOCABULARY WORDS @ ADAH

1. Ad hoc -

2. Syncretism -

3. Administer -

4. Valor –

5. Sanctioned -

6. Fidelity –

7. Admonish –

8. Irrevocable –

9. Unqualifiable -

10. Bewail -

RUTH TEST

1. Ruth is the wife's degree? T/F

2. Ruth is a descendant of Jephthah? T/F

3. Ruth was an Ammonite? T/F

4. Ruth was 80 years old when she met Boaz? T/F

5. When ___ ___ was the Ambassador to the Court of France, he attended a gathering of the literati of Paris. He was asked for a reading, and he took a manuscript out of his pocket and read the entire book of Ruth.

6. Because of their idolatry, the Moabites became an abomination unto God and stayed that way until Ruth met Boaz on the threshing floor in Gilead. T/F

7. Who was Ruth's first husband? Why did they get a divorce?

8. Who was Ruth's grandfather?

9. Who was Ruth's Father? How did he get killed?

10. Who was Naomi? How was she related to Ruth?

11. What does Naomi mean?

12. What did Naomi change her name to? Why?

13. What does Ruth Rabbah 2:20 say Orpah did after she left Naomi?

14. After a long day's work, Ruth had __ handfuls of barley.

15. Who was Boaz?

16. Who were his parents?

17. What did Ruth's husband's next of kin give Boaz?

18. What was Ruth and Boaz's sons' name?

19. Which Heroine is Ruth related to? How are they related?

20. What is Ruth's pass? Who gave it to her?

ESTHER TEST

1. What does the name Esther mean?

2. Who reared Esther?

3. In what country did the story of Esther take place?

4. What other two biblical characters lived there?

5. In what year was the Book of Esther written? Who was the author?

6. What was Esther's birth name?

7. What is peculiar about the book of Esther?

8. Who was King Xerxes' queen before Esther?

9. Why was the previous queen dethroned and banished from the palace?

10. What is Mordecai's relationship to Esther? Explain

11. Who was Haman?

12. Who caused the edict to go forth that all Jews be extirpated?

13. What happened to Haman?

14. What position did Mordecai hold?

15. What does the name Hadassah mean?

16. How long was the preparation period for maidens who were to go before the king?

17. What made Haman so angry with Mordecai?

18. What did Mordecai do when he learned of the edict to destroy the Jews?

19. Who pleaded with Esther to go before the king to save her people?

20. How long did Esther fast before going before the king?

21. What is the color of this degree?

22. What is the flower of this degree?

23. What present-day feast celebrates Esther's victory for her people?

24. What is Esther's beatitude?

25. What is Esther's emblem?

26. What is Esther's jewel?

27. What does the crown and scepter signify?

28. Who gave Esther her pass?

29. How many chapters are in the book of Esther?

30. What was Esther's father's name?

31. Which Heroine is Esther related to? Explain

32. Explain the beef between Mordecai and Haman

33. How many feet are fifty cubits?

34. How much is 10,000 talents of silver in USD?

35. What country did King Xerxes invade?

MARTHA TEST

1. Where can the story of Martha be found?

2. Where was Martha born?

3. Who were the other members of her family?

4. Where did they live?

5. What did Martha do when she heard Jesus was coming across the mountains?

6. What does the sign that she gave Jesus represent?

7. What is the shortest scripture in the bible?

8. How long was Lazarus dead when Jesus came?

9. Where did Martha go when she left Judah?

10. Where did Lazarus go? What did he do there?

11. What did the people of Tarascon ask Martha to do?

12. What did she do before she approached the dragon?

13. While in Tarascon, Martha converted many people to Judaism. T/F

ELECTA TEST

1. Who is Electa?

2. In what scripture can you find the story of Electa?

3. Who wrote a heartfelt letter to The Elect Lady and her children warning them to beware of false prophets and not to be guilty of associating with them?

4. Who was St John the Evangelist?

5. What did he advise Electa to do?

6. For what was she known around the country of Judah?

7. ___ ___ went to Electa's home demanding that she renounce her Christian faith, but she refused.

8. What happened to her when she refused?

9. How long was Electa in prison?

10. After serving one year in prison, she was given another opportunity, but she refused. What happened to her then?

11. What services did she offer in her mansion?

12. What did she say when she was about to expire?

13. Why did the ruling authorities fear the Christians?

14. What did the Romans do to coerce them to renounce their Christian faith?

15. How old was St John the Evangelist?

LANDMARKS VOCABULARY WORDS

1. Landmark -

2. Fidelity –

3. 3. Constancy –

4. 4. Beneficent –

5. Labyrinth –

6. Obligations –

7. Inviolably –

8. Amenable –

9. Prerogative –

10. Dispensation –

LANDMARKS TEST

1) What is a Landmark?

2) How many Landmarks are there?

3) What scripture can the lesson on the sister's degree be found?

4) Which heroine's lessons can be found in the Old Testament?

5) What are Adah's moral virtues?

6) What are the purposes of the Order of The Eastern Star?

7) Name three benefits you receive by being a part of the Order.

8) A candidate must believe in Jesus to be eligible for membership. T/F

9) What is a Supreme Being?

10) What are the modes of recognition?

11) If you become inactive in the Order, can you tell its secrets to nonmembers? Explain why or why not?

12) What is a Covenant?

Order In The Order

13) Control of the Rite lies in the SubordinateChapter of the Adoptive Rite? T/F

14) Who appoints officers that are not elected?

15) Can a Chapter have an Initiation without a Master Mason present? Which Landmark is it?

16) If you steal money from your Chapter and then join a Chapter in another jurisdiction, can your previous Chapter try you for the offense? Which Landmark is it?

17) The Worthy Matron writes an amendment to the by-laws saying she is entitled to a $1500 monthly stipend from the Chapter. The Chapter disagrees with it and tries to discuss it with her and the Worthy Patron to no avail, what must the Chapter do? Which Landmark is it?

18) Which Landmark gives the Grand Matron the authority to grant dispensations?

19) How is the Grand Patron escorted to the East and by whom? FULL AND COMPLETE ANSWERS ONLY!!!

20) What is a dispensation?

21) How often should each Chapter elect new officers?

22) Who presides over Elections?

23) Your boyfriend/husband's sidepiece is a member of another Chapter in your jurisdiction. You have several relatives in that Chapter, and they all permitted you to attend their meeting. You and other members of your Chapter decided y'all are going to her meeting to confront her. You are current on your dues and show up at their meeting in full regalia. All y'all pass the Recognition Test and your relatives vouch

for y'all. Should you be admitted into their meeting? Why or why not? FULL AND COMPLETE ANSWERS ONLY!!! Which Landmark is it?

BEATITUDES TEST

1. What are Beatitudes?

2. How many Beatitudes are there?

3. What Scripture can they be found?

4. Who was Jesus preaching to and where? 5. At what point in Jesus' ministry was Sermon on the Mount preached?

6. What is the meaning of the word Beatitude? What is its origin?

7. Each Beatitude is composed of two parts, what are they?

8. What is the condition in Electa's Beatitude?

9. What is the Result in Adah's Beatitude?

10. What is Martha's Beatitude?

11. How is it associated with her?

12. What does the word meek mean?

13. Which Beatitude was highly praised by Mahatma Gandhi?

ANSWERS - BRAIN TEASER TUESDAY

1. The Five Degrees of the Order of the Eastern Star are founded on the Holy Scriptures.

2. Whose badge of office are the crossed pens within the Star? Secretary

3. Whose duty is it to guard and protect the interests of the Chapter? Chair of Trustees

4. Who makes the first impression upon a Candidate? Conductress

5. Whose emblem is the Baton within the Star? Associate Conductress

6. What do two blows of the gavel do? Calls up the officers.

7. What do the five distinct raps at the door represent? The 5 Heroines

8. Who invites the Worthy Matron and other officers into the Chapter room? Associate Conductress

9. When can a member's Badge be reversed? For mourning purposes

10. Whose jewel is the Crossed Batons within a Star? Marshal

11. According to the Ritual, there are **three** places where a burial ceremony can be held,

what are they? Church, cemetery, or house of the deceased

12. According to the Ritual, which two officers can be compensated if approved before elections? Secretary and Sentinel

13. What is the Special Motto? Fairest Among Thousands Altogether Lovely

14. Which flag takes precedence over all others? Christian

15. Which heroine said, "Lord if thou hadst been here, my brother had not died?" Martha Who was her brother Lazarus

16. Which Heroine went to jail and for how long? Electa. One year

17. The illustration below is on the first page of your Ritual. It's very enlightening and filled with symbolism. Identify each sign and/or symbol in each section…There's a total of 14. See illustration.

18. Whose Emblem was changed? Electa. What was it originally and what is it now? It was the Grip and the Cup. Now it's just the cup.

19. Where was Jephthah when asked to be the leader of the army? In the land of Tob

20. Which three Heroines make up the Triangle of Battle? Adah, Esther, and Electa. Why were they chosen? There was a battle in each of their stories and together they formed a triangle on the Star point.

Order In The Order

21. Who painted the first OES Signet? Robert Morris' daughter

22. What is Mount Sylvan Academy? Dr Robert Morris was the principal and teacher there. Where is it located? Oxford Mississippi

23. When and where was the first Eastern Star Chapter formed? December 28, 1868. NY What was the name of it? Alpha #1

24. What is the proper way to sit in the Chapter room? With your feet flat on the floor and your knees together.

25. Is it proper to sit with your legs crossed? No. They can be crossed at the ankles.

26. I am an elevated stone or tablet on which sacrifices were offered, what am I? Altar

27. When the Bible is open on the Altar, it creates a Holy area between the prepared Altar and the East, and no one is permitted to pass between these two places.

28. While she was expiring and about to pass to a better land, she prayed with her dying breath: Father, forgive them, for they know not what they do! Who is she? Electa

29. I am from Moab. I am a descendant of Lot. Who am I? Ruth

30. What did Naomi say to call her and why? Mara. Because she was bitter.

31. Match the Central Division of the Star with the Heroine:

    Refulgent Sun- Esther

    Lily of the Valley- Ruth

    Lamb and a Cross- Martha

    Lion- Electa

Open Bible- Adah

32. Match the flower with the heroine.

Violet- Adah

White Lily- Esther

Red Rose- Electa

Yellow Jasmine- Ruth

The Fern- Martha

33. I am known as the Lady of High Repute in the land of Judea. I was born to a noble family. Who am I? Electa

ANSWERS - HISTORICAL SKETCH TEST

1. What year was the Rite of Adoption Established? 1774

2. Who established it? Grand Orient of France

3. What is the Grand Orient? Grand Lodge

4. What is the Grand East? Seat of the Grand Master in the Grand Lodge

5. What year was Adoptive Masonry established in France? 1775

6. What year was Adoptive Masonry established in Holland? 1801

7. When was it dissolved? June 10, 1810

8. How many degrees did it consist of? 4

9. Name the degrees and explain each one. Apprentice, Companion, Mistress and Perfect Mistress

10. What did the fourth degree symbolize? The passage of men from the world of change and discord to a pure land of rest and peace

11. Name the Nine officers of the Lodge of Adoption. Grand Master, Grand Mistress,

Orator, Inspector, Inspectress, Depositor, Depositrix, Conductor and Conductress

12. The room was divided into four sections, what did they represent? The four corners of the earth

13. For whom were the two thrones erected in the East? Grand Master and Grand Mistress

14. Who is the Father of French Masonry? M Boubee

15. What did he say was the biggest event in Adoptive Masonry? When Empress Josephine was installed as Grand Mistress

16. The ceremonies of the Lodge were borrowed from whom? Coal burners

17. What year was the Adoptive Rite introduced in the US? 1850

18. Where did they borrow the idea of formulating the degrees? French Grand Orient

ANSWERS - ROBERT MORRIS TEST

1. What was Robert Morris' birth name? Robert Williams Peckham

2. When and where was Robert Morris born? August 31, 1818 – 26 Rector St NY

3. Where did he get the last name Morris? His foster father John Morris

4. When and where did he receive Masonic Light? March 5, 1846. Oxford Lodge. Oxford MS

5. When did he become a Master Mason? July 3, 1846

6. When did he become a Heroine of Jericho? 1847

7. Who hired him to become Principal @ Eureka Masonic College? Holmes County Masons

8. Where is Eureka Masonic College? Richland MS What is it also known as? Little Red Schoolhouse

9. What is the birthplace of The Eastern Star? Little Red Schoolhouse

10. When and where did Robert Morris give his first lecture? November 1850. Collierville TN

11. What were the Heroines called during the Constellation Period? Correspondents

12. What was the Cabalistic Motto called during that period? Fairest Among Ten Thousands and Altogether Lovely

13. Who was Electa during the Constellation Period? Areme

14. What was the name of the first Constellation? Purity Constellation #1

15. What year was the Supreme Constellation of the Eastern Star formed? 1855

16. What year was the Constellation Period discontinued? 1860

17. What was the second period called? Family System

18. What was the name of the first Family? Miriam Family #111 what state were they from? Illinois what year were they founded? 1866

19. What were the Correspondent's names changed to? Adah, Ruth, Esther, Martha, and Electa

20. What was the Cabalistic Motto changed to? Fairest Among Thousands Altogether Lovely

21. What year was the first Ritual printed? 1865

22. What was it called? Rosary of the Eastern Star

23. What year was the Family Period discontinued? 1868

24. Who did Dr Robert Morris transfer control to? Robert Macoy What year? 1868

25. Where did Dr Morris travel to? The Holy Land

26. What did he do while he was there? Formed the first Lodge in the Holy Land

27. What system was formed after The Family Period? The Chapter System

28. What was the name of the first Chapter? Alpha #1 When and where was it formed? December 28, 1868, NY Who was the first OES Candidate? Robert Macoy's wife Mrs. Eliza A. Macoy

29. What's the difference between a Rite and an Order? An Order has a form of government with elected officers and by-laws. Neither the Constellation System nor the Family System had elected officers

30. The Eastern Star is divided into three eras, what are they?

I.   1850-1868 under the leadership of Dr Robert Morris.

II. 1868-1876 Rob Macoy - Chapter/Grand Chapter was formed.

III. 1876-present General Grand Chapter was founded by Willis Engle of Indiana

31. What was the first Black Chapter? Queen Esther Chapter # 1. When and where was it started? December 1, 1874 in Washington DC. Who was the first Black WM and WP? Sister Martha Welch and Brother Thornton A Jackson

32. What opened as a Grand Lodge of Adoption and closed as a Grand Chapter of the Order of the Eastern Star? Grand Chapter of Michigan

Bonus Questbion

B1. Why do you think Dr Morris' first two systems were unsuccessful? He was a one-man show with no structure.

ANSWERS - ADAH TEST

1. How many times is the name "Adah" entioned in the scripture? 0

2. What does Adah mean? Ornament

3. Where does the story take place? Gilead

4. What is Adah's emblem(s)? Sword and Veil

5. Who is Jephthah? He was a resident of Gilead, the son of Gilead and a harlot AKA prostitute, and the 9th Judge.

6. How many years did he serve as Judge? 6 years

7. Name two roles of a Judge? 1) A Judge was the highest governing official in the nation. 2) They acted as military leaders in times of trial.

8. How many Judges were there? 13 What # Judge was Jephthah? 9

9. Who was the first Judge? Othniel, Caleb's nephew

10. Who was the first female Judge? Deborah What number was she? 4

11. Who were Jephthah's parents? Gilead and a prostitute

12. Why did his brothers kick him out of the house? They said he made the whole family look bad. They called him a reject and a "Child of Shame because his mother was a prostitute.

13. Why didn't his father try to stop them? He was dead.

14. Where was Jephthah's home? Gilead

15. Where was he when the elders came to him? In the land of Tob

16. Jephthah's selection as Leader and Judge was a 3-fold consideration. What was the process? 1. He was selected by the Elders. 2. He was approved by the people. 3. He was sanctioned by God.

17. What is Adah's pass? Alas, my daughter!

18. By whom was it given? Jephthah

19. What vow did Jephthah make to the Lord? He said, "Lord if thou shall without fail deliver the children of Ammon into mine hands, then it shall be that whatsoever cometh forth of the doors of my house to meet me when I return from the children of Ammon, shall surely be the Lord's and I will offer it up for a burnt offering."

20. How many brothers and sisters did Adah have? 0

21. Why did Adah bewail her virginity? 1. Every Jewish maiden wanted to be the mother of the Messiah. 2. After she was executed there would be no heir because she was the only child.

22. How long did Adah stay in the mountains? Two months

23. Together the sword and veil represent what? Right and Revelation

24. In the book of Revelation, the throne of God was separated from the rest of the heavenly court by what? A veil

25. What is the Christ symbol of this degree? Open bible

26. What season does Adah represent? Spring

27. What is her beatitude? Blessed are the pure in heart for they shall see God.

28. In what scripture can you find the story of Jephthah's Daughter? Judges 11

ANSWERS - RUTH TEST

1. Ruth is the wife's degree? T/F

2. Ruth is a descendant of Jephthah? T/F

3. Ruth was an Ammonite? T/F

4. Ruth was 80 years old when she met Boaz? T/F

5. When Benjamin Franklin was the Ambassador to the Court of France, he attended a gathering of the literati of Paris. He was asked for a reading, and he took a manuscript out of his pocket and read the entire book of Ruth.

6. Because of their idolatry, the Moabites became an abomination unto God and stayed that way until Ruth met Boaz on the threshing floor in Gilead. T/F She met him on the threshing floor in Bethlehem.

7. Who was Ruth's first husband? Mahlon Why did they get a divorce? They didn't get a divorce, he died.

8. Who was Ruth's grandfather? King Balak

9. Who was Ruth's Father? King Eglon How did he get killed? He was stabbed to

death by Judge Ehud

10. Who was Naomi? Ruth's mother-in-law

11. What does Naomi mean? Sweetness

12. What did Naomi change her name to? Mara Why? She said, "Do not call me Naomi, call me Mara, for the Almighty has dealt very bitterly with me." Mara means bitter.

13. What does Ruth Rabbah 2:20 say Orpah did after she left Naomi? She slept with 100 men and a dog in one night.

14. After a long day's work, Ruth had two handfuls of barley.

15. Who was Boaz? Boaz was the richest man in Bethlehem, a well-known and charitable man.

16. Who were his parents? He was the son of a harlot named Rahab and Salmon (Elimelech's brother).

17. What did Ruth's husband's next of kin give Boaz? A shoe

18. What was Ruth and Boaz's sons' name? Obed

19. Which Heroine is Ruth related to? Esther, How are they related? Ruth was Esther's great-greatgreat aunt.

20. What is Ruth's pass? Who is this, who gave it to her? Boaz

ANSWERS - ESTHER TEST

1. What does the name Esther mean? Esther is an Old Persian word that means Star.

2. Who reared Esther? Mordecai

3. In what country did the story of Esther take place? Susa (Capital of Persia)

4. What other two biblical characters lived there? Daniel and Nehemiah

5. In what year was the Book of Esther written? Between 492 BC and 460 BC, Who was the author? Unknown

6. What was Esther's birth name? Hadassah

7. What is peculiar about the book of Esther? It never mentions God's name

8. Who was King Xerxes' queen before Esther? Queen Vashti

9. Why was the previous queen dethroned and banished from the palace? He felt she disobeyed and humiliated him.

10. What is Mordecai's relationship to Esther? Cousin

11. Who was Haman? Haman was an Amalekite, the son of Hammedatha. He was the king's favorite who became the Prime Minister. He hated Jews, especially Mordecai. He offered to pay 10,000 talents of silver to have them extirpated after Mordecai refused to bow to him.

12. Who caused the edict to go forth that all Jews be extirpated? Haman

13. What happened to Haman? He was hung on the gallows he had prepared for the Mordecai.

14. What position did Mordecai hold? He was the gatekeeper of the courtyard. He later ruled the estate that King Xeres gave Esther.

15. What does the name Hadassah mean? Myrtle

16. How long was the preparation period for maidens who were to go before the king? One year

17. When was Esther crowned queen?

18. What made Haman so angry with Mordecai? He refused to bow to him. Haman felt like he disrespected him.

19. What did Mordecai do when he learned of the edict to destroy the Jews? He tore his clothes in anguish and put on sackcloth with ashes then went out into the middle of the city and cried out to the Lord. Then he went to the gates of the king's palace to tell Esther

20. Who pleaded with Esther to go before the king to save her people? Mordecai

21. How long did Esther fast before going before the king? Three days

22. What is the color of this degree? White

23. What is the flower of this degree? White lily

24. What present-day feast celebrates Esther's victory for her people? Feast of Purim

25. What is Esther's beatitude? Blessed are the peacemakers for they shall be called the children of God.

26. What is Esther's emblem? Crown and Scepter

27. What is Esther's jewel? Diamond

28. What does the crown and scepter signify? A crown and scepter united represent forces of power and authority welded together to ensure justice for all.

29. Who gave Esther her pass? King Xerxes

30. How many chapters are in the book of Esther?

31. What was Esther's father's name? Abihail

32. Which Heroine is Esther related to? Ruth

33. Explain the beef between Mordecai and Haman. Haman and Mordecai's beef dates to the times when Saul was King of Israel. Haman, the son of Hammedatha the Amalekite hated Jews. The Amalekites attacked Israel when they came out of Egypt, so God told Saul through the prophet Samuel to attack the Amalekites and destroy everything that belonged to them: men, women, children, infants, cattle, sheep, donkeys, and camels. (1 Samuel 15) Saul attacked the Amalekites but spared the life of Agag their king. Saul's disobedience caused discord between the Benjamites and Amalekites. Aside from the historical beef, Haman was jealous of Mordecai.

34. How many feet are 50 cubits? 75

35. How much is 10,000 talents of silver in USD? $12M

36. What country did King Xerxes invade? Greece

ANSWERS - MARTHA TEST

1. Where can the story of Martha be found? John 11 and Luke 10:38-42

2. Where was Martha born? Judah, modern-day Israel

3. Who were the other members of her family? Her brother Lazarus, and her sister Mary

4. Where did they live? Bethany

5. What did Martha do when she heard Jesus was coming across the mountains? She ran to him, fell on her knees, and said, "Lord, if thou hadst been here, my brother had not died. But I know that even now, whatsoever thou wilt ask of God he will give it to thee.

6. What does the sign that she gave Jesus represent? The perfect triangle: the holy trinity which represents God the Father, the one who rules, God the Son, the creator of all things, and God the Holy Ghost, the completer of all material things.

7. What is the shortest scripture in the bible? John 11:35 – Jesus wept.

8. How long was Lazarus dead when Jesus came? Four days

9. Where did Martha go when she left Judah? Provence (Southeast France)

10. Where did Lazarus go? Kiton, Cyprus. What did he do there? He was appointed bishop by Paul and Barnabas.

11. What did the people of Tarascon ask Martha to do? They knew that Martha was close friends with Jesus and was filled with the Holy Ghost, so they asked her to contain the dragon.

12. What did she do before she approached the dragon? Martha fasted and prayed daily. She only ate once a day and prayed 100 times during the day and 100 times during the night.

13. While in Tarascon, Martha converted many people to Judaism. T/F

ANSWERS - ELECTA TEST

1. Who is Electa? The Ideal Mother was an educated lady of high repute and strong convictions.

2. In what scripture can you find the story of Electa? 2 John

3. Who wrote a heartfelt letter to The Elect Lady and her children warning them to beware of false prophets and not to be guilty of associating with them? St John the Evangelist

4. Who was St John the Evangelist? One of the Christian church's most revered and recognized authorities

5. What did he warn The Elect Lady and her children to do? Beware of false prophets and not to be guilty of associating with them.

6. What was Electa known around the country of Judah for? Her philanthropy and benevolence.

7. Roman Soldiers went to Electa's home demanding that she renounce her Christian faith but she refused.

8. What happened to her when she refused? She and her entire family were dragged to prison for one year.

9. How long was Electa in prison? One year

10. After serving one year in prison, she was given another opportunity, but she refused. What happened to her then? She and her entire family were crucified.

11. What services did she offer in her mansion? She ran a homeless shelter.

12. What did she say when she was about to expire? "Forgive them Father for they know not what they do!"

13. Why did the ruling authorities fear the Christians? The ruling authorities feared the Christians would rebel and make them lose their power.

14. What did the Romans do to coerce them to renounce their Christian faith? They threatened Christians with abuse, imprisonment, and death.

15. How old was St John the Evangelist? 90

ANSWERS – LANDMARKS TEST

1. What is a Landmark? Landmarks are a set of principles, ancient and unchangeable precepts or rules.

2. How many Landmarks are there? 15

3. What scripture can the lesson on the sister's degree be found? John 11 and Luke 10:38-42

4. Which heroine's lessons can be found in the Old Testament? Adah, Ruth, and Esther

5. What are Adah's moral virtues? Integrity (fidelity)

6. What are the purposes of the Order of The Eastern Star? Comfort, protect, and aid each other in our journey through the Labyrinth of human life. 7) Name three benefits you receive by being a part of the Order. Social privileges, support, friendship (Brotherhood/Sisterhood) love, protection, welfare of Sisters secured by Brotherhood, respect, knowledge, advice in misfortune, sympathy in time of sorrow, aid in time of distress, etc.

7. A candidate must believe in Jesus to be eligible for membership. T/<u>F</u>

8. What is a Supreme Being? Higher authority; God, Yahweh, Allah, Jehovah, etc.

9. What are the modes of recognition? Signs, pass, and grip

10. If you become inactive in the Order, can you tell its secrets to nonmembers? No Explain why or why not? A covenant of secrecy voluntarily assumed is perpetual; from the force of such obligation, there is no possibility of release. Even if you become an inactive member of the Order, you are still obligated to live by and remember your oath of obligation. Never talk OES to non-members.

11. What is a Covenant? An agreement of promise between two or more parties.

12. Control of the Rite lies in the Subordinate Chapter of the Adoptive Rite. T/<u>F</u>

13. Who appoints officers that are not elected? Worthy Matron

14. Can a Chapter have an Initiation without a Master Mason present? No Which Landmark is it? 9

15. If you steal money from your Chapter and then join a Chapter in another jurisdiction, can your previous Chapter try you for the offense? Yes. Which Landmark is it? 10

16. The Worthy Matron writes an amendment to the by-laws saying she is entitled to a $1500 monthly stipend from the Chapter. The Chapter disagrees with it and tries to discuss it with her and the Worthy Patron to no avail, what must the Chapter do? Which Landmark is it? 11

17. Which Landmark gives the Grand Matron the authority to grant dispensations? None. #12 gives the Grand Patron the authority to grant dispensations.

18. How is the Grand Patron escorted to the East and by whom? WM gives three gavel raps, Chapter gives the Grand Honors sign, and he is escorted to the East by Conductress in the South or the Marshal.

19. What is a dispensation? A system of rules for governing affairs. An official exemption from a law or obligation.

20. How often should each Chapter elect new officers? Annually

21. Who presides over Elections? Worthy Patron, Past Patron, or a Grand Officer

22. Your boyfriend/husband's sidepiece is a member of another Chapter in your jurisdiction. You have several relatives in that Chapter, and they all permitted you to attend their meeting. You and other members of your Chapter decided y'all are going to her meeting to confront her. You are current on your dues and show up at their meeting in full regalia. All of y'all pass the Recognition Test and your relatives vouch for y'all. Should you be admitted into their meeting? No Why or why not? Per Landmark 15. Every member may visit and sit in every regular Chapter, except when such visitor is likely to disturb the harmony or interrupt the progress of the Chapter he or she proposes to visit.

ANSWERS - BEATITUDES TEST

1. What are Beatitudes? -- Set of teachings by Jesus @ Sermon on the Mount. It was Jesus' longest recorded Sermon; it lasted several days Beatitude comes from the Latin word "beatus" which means happy, fortunate, or blissful.

2. How many Beatitudes are there? 8

3. What Scripture can they be found? Matthew 5

4. Where was Jesus preaching? On a hillside by Capernaum

5. At what point in Jesus' ministry was Sermon on the Mount preached? Early, after he was baptized by John the Baptist

6. What is the meaning of the word Beatitude? Happy, fortunate, or blissful. What is its origin? It comes from the Latin word "beatus "

7. Each Beatitude is composed of two parts, what are they? Condition and Result

8. What is the condition in Electa's Beatitude? Blessed are they which are persecuted for righteous sake.

9. What is the Result of Adah's Beatitude? For they shall see God

10. What is Martha's Beatitude? Blessed are they that mourn for they shall be comforted

11. How is it associated with her? She mourned the death of her brother Lazarus

12. What does the word "meek" mean? Those who submit to God's authority; God's children will inherit everything}

13. Which Beatitude was highly praised by Mahatma Ghandi? Blessed are the Meek, for they shall inherit the earth

Outro

WHAT IS A VIRTUOUS WOMAN?

According to dictionary.com, the definition of the word virtue is behavior showing high moral standards. Proverbs 31:10 says that her price is far above rubies. A virtuous woman is a noble upstanding woman with honor, dignity, loyalty, and worthiness. The five Heroines represented in the Order of the Eastern Star were all virtuous women.

Adah, the daughter was a virtuous woman. She was loyal to her father and assured that he kept his vow.

She is described in Proverbs 31:29, "Many daughters have done virtuously, but thou excellest them all."

Ruth, the widow was a virtuous woman. She is described in Proverbs 31:31, "Give her of the fruit of her hands; and let her own works praise her in the gates." Proverbs 31:28 Her children arise up, and call her blessed; her husband also, and he praiseth her. Proverbs 31:23 – Her husband is known in the gates when he sitteth among the elders of the land.

Proverbs 31:14 – She is like the merchants' ships; she bringeth her food from afar.

Esther, the wife's degree was a virtuous woman. She was a Jewish damsel who married

King Xerxes and then saved her people from extirpation.

Proverbs 31:30 best describes her, "Favour is deceitful, and beauty is vain: but a woman that feareth the Lord, she shall be praised." Proverbs 31:23 also describes her, "Her husband is known in the gates when he sitteth among the elders of the land. Proverbs 31:26, "She openeth her mouth with wisdom; and in her tongue is the law of kindness.

Proverbs 31:11, "The heart of her husband doth safely trust in her so that he shall no need of spoil."

Martha, the sister's degree was a virtuous woman.

She, her sister Mary, and her brother Lazarus were Jesus' close friends. It was in her home that he found comfort. Proverbs 31:27 best describes her,

"She looketh well to the way of her household, and eateth not the bread of idleness.

Electa, the mother's degree was a virtuous woman. She was loyal and refused to deny her Christian faith. She opened her home to those in need.

Proverbs 31:20 best describes her, "She stretched out her hand to the poor; she reacheth forth her hands to the needy."

Thank you for your purchase and I hope you were enlightened.

With Love, Past Worthy Matron Tanya Rice

DISCLAIMER

THE NEXT SECTION IS GRAPHIC AND MAY NOT BE SUITABLE FOR THE WEAK

AT HEART OR THOSE WHO CAN'T STAND THE TRUTH!

IT'S RATED XXX SO YOU'RE MORE THAN WELCOME TO LEAVE NOW! THE STUDY SESSION IS OVER SO READ AT YOUR OWN

RISK!!!

XXXXXXXXXXXXXXXXX

ORDER IN THE ORDER

Sisters, if you are still here, I assume you're enjoying this study session thus far. Thank you for your time and I hope you learned a thing or two along the way.

We've covered my journey into the Order, the History of the Adoptive Rite, Robert Morris, the Five Heroines, you heard Esther sing, (lol), Landmarks, Beatitudes, and a few other things. Heck, we even went to a family reunion. Pat yourself on the back if those Brain Teaser Tuesdays didn't fry your brain.

The study session is over and it's too cold in Rockford to return to Levings Lake Park. It was 82 degrees outside when we started, now it's 8 below zero. Girl, this weather is bipolar, I swear.

Now that we got that out of the way, let's take a girl's trip down to Houston Texas. It's time to stand on bitness - **grown folk bitness**! Parental discretion is advised from this point on. Names have been withheld to protect the guilty.

Our Uber driver Anna Mae Beasley has finally arrived. Child, where is this chick going in this 67 Pinto! Jesus take the wheel! Please say a prayer for us as we journey back to Houston, SMDH! If you can't stand the truth, you might want to stay outta this raggedy-ass Pinto because honey, it's about to get real.

The title of this book is Order in the Order. What is order? According to dictionary.com, order is defined as the formal arrangement of things. Order is a situation in which everything is arranged in its proper place. The synonym of order is structure.

This is what we're going to discuss today, order and lack thereof.

The Order of the Eastern Star is a charitable organization designed to comfort, protect, and aid our sisters and brothers in our journey through the Labyrinth of Human Life. However, it appears to be a big party, bigger than the Grand Feast and the Splendid Feast held by King Xerxes combined!

I was inactive in the Order for seven years, but when I became active again, I noticed a shift in the organization. The sisterly bond has dissipated. I've attended OES events where the vibe in the room was so hate-filled that you could cut the tension with a knife. The sexual energy was so overwhelming I couldn't determine if I had pissed, started my period, or nut in my panties. I didn't feel the warmth of sisterhood anywhere in the air. The order has left the Order and after careful observations, I see why.

The Order is now comprised of ladies who weren't accepted into sororities while in college, combined with ladies who never held a position in their lives, combined with ladies who didn't have friends growing up, combined with ladies looking for a man to fuck. What a lethal combination. Excuse my French but I told y'all that we're going to stand on **grown folk bitness**! You still have time to leave.

Notice I said ladies and not sisters. The Sisterhood has left the organization and there are no requirements to join anymore, it's no longer reserved for the wives, daughters, sisters, mothers, and widows of Master Masons. If you have $35 and a wet pussy, you can become a member of the Chapter of your choice.

Sadly, community service has been replaced with parties and the cover charge for the party is a bottle of Hennessy and a double-edged sword to stab your sister in the back. Grand Session has become a fundraiser and a Grand Orgy. Truth be told, you can call it a Diddy Freak Off without Diddy himself but a few impersonators. There's nothing wrong with people partying and having a good time but there's a time and place for everything. Oftentimes, it's not what you do but how you do it.

Ladies, I'm talking to you, not the "Sisters." My question is, why and how do you have the audacity to sit in that Chapter room, hug, and call someone your sister but before the Worthy Matron says farewell and sounds the gavel, you're in bed with her husband? Don't answer that question, just let it marinate.

Some ladies are so bold, promiscuous, and trifling that when their best friend in their chapter has a baby, they embrace the baby and train them to call her auntie but deep down inside, she really wants to be the baby's stepmother.

I know that some of y'all may not have any home training, or you might not know anything about family values but when I look at my brothers, I see a brother, a friend, a protector, and a confidant. I agree that we might be closer to some brothers than others but they're still our brothers at the end of the day. Whatever the case may be, our brothers are our brothers, and they should be respected as such. If there are any brothers in our midst, we expect reciprocity!

Some of y'all ladies lust over every brother with a dime in his pocket and a bulge in his pants. Y'all don't realize it but in some cases, that dime is all he has to his name and some of those bulges might be blue balls from his wife not having sex with him because he infected her with an STD. Momma used to say everything that looks good to you ain't always good for you, take heed.

Order In The Order

If your flesh is that weak to the point where you can't sit your horny ass in the Chapter with a Worthy Patron without having sex with him because you think he has a few coins in his pocket, you probably need to check yourself.

This is a **volunteer** organization. According to Webster's Dictionary, the word volunteer is defined as the act of rendering selfless service to a cause, oftentimes for free and without coercion. If anyone coerced you to join this organization, both of y'all need to demit expeditiously!

On that note, being a volunteer organization, no one should be paid a six-figure salary or any salary at all for that matter. However, according to page 183 in your Ritual, the only officers who are entitled to be compensated are the Secretary and Sentinel. When was the last time you heard of either of them being compensated? Asking for a friend.

We are a charitable organization after all. Fundraisers should be for a specific purpose to which the entire jurisdiction should be privy to. For example, if the Grand body decides the jurisdiction should sell sweet potato pies to purchase a building for everyone to meet, communication should be sent out via the Grand Chapter. The funds should be deposited into the **Grand Chapter's** bank account, not into someone's pocket. The entire jurisdiction should be aware of the goal and progress of the building fund, right? Right!

However, there are jurisdictions doing fundraiser after fundraiser and no one knows how much money was collected or where the monies went. Twenty years later they don't even have a doorknob for the building. Does anyone else smell a rat? If you don't maybe you're part of the problem.

Now let's talk about title whores. What is a title whore? A title whore is someone who will do ANYTHING and I do mean ANYTHING for a title, rather it's Grand Matron,

Associate Grand Matron, Worthy Matron, Associate Matron, etc. Get my drift? Ladies, I hate to be the bearer of bad news but outside of this illustrious organization, no one knows what a Grand Matron or any of the positions above are, so don't sell your soul or your ass for those positions. Last time I checked, those positions don't pay a damn thing unless you have sticky fingers. People don't care about your title; they care about your character!

If you get voted out of a position guess what? Your bills are still going to get paid (unless they weren't getting paid beforehand) so hold your head up high and continue to let your light shine. Don't walk around the labyrinth spewing rhetoric, gossiping, and throwing jabs at the chapter you loved more than life itself when they elected you.

When my mother was a member of this organization, I used to hear her and her sisters on the phone discussing their private lives. They used to have a bond so close that she never discussed the previous conversation when she talked to the next sister. The ladies today are different. Before they get off the phone good, they call everyone who will listen and discuss everything the last person talked about and even more. This is one reason why I advised y'all to read and live by page 93 in your Ritual.

Associate Matrons, lemme holla at y'all for a minute or two. An Associate Matron is supposed to be a reflection of her Worthy Matron, as the sun rises in the east and sets in the west. She is *supposed* to be the right hand of her Worthy Matron, her backbone, her ride-or-die. If the Worthy Matron is absent, her Associate Matron sits in the East. Notice I said in her **absence,** not her presence.

Associate Matrons, please stay in your lane. Please stop sitting in the West trying to control and sabotage the East, and don't sit in the West plotting and backstabbing your way to the East, that's Adah's sword, not yours! That's not a good look, remember what goes around comes around Associate Matrons. Cousin Karma is ruthless, and she doesn't have a conscious. That bitch will sneak up on you like a thief in the night! Associate Matrons beware, heavy is the head that wears the crown, and that crown looks light as a feather until you put it on and it knocks you to your knees.

There's something about that seat in the West where some ladies sit in it and desperately feel the need to get to the East. They will rob, steal, and kill to get there. Sometimes I wonder what kind of cologne the Worthy Patron wears that makes the AM want to get close to him. Mine used to smell like badussy and old spice. LoL, I'm kidding WP, calm down, but you did used to be musty, and you smelled like Grandmama's mothballs. LoL

They spend years backstabbing and dogging their Worthy Matron trying to get to the East but when they reach their destination, they don't last three months! Don't chase the position, let the position chase you because the catch isn't always worth the chase. I'm just saying, you heard it right here on Channel 357 WPWM news at noon.

Ladies, we need to go back to the days when we respected ourselves and those around us, this foolishness in the "order" of the Eastern Star must cease! Stop letting those brothers play pass the pussy with you because all they'll do is fuck you and then talk about you during and after their lodge meetings. I almost forgot to mention all those "sexy" pics y'all keep sending to the brothers, keep in mind that you're just a one-night stand or a sidepiece- if you've elevated to that status.

Those brothers have show and tell with your pics and they laugh and talk about y'all like a dog. I overheard one brother talking about how easy a particular lady was, he said her pussy stank and it looked like she took that dusty wig off her head and put it in her panties. My gawd, did y'all forget that some of these brothers gossip more than women?

We're casting a negative light on ourselves then we get in our feelings when the world

Tanya Rice

judges us.

While we're talking about respect, do you address your doctor, Michelle Washington as Michelle, or Dr Washington? Do you address your attorney as Michelle or Attorney Washington? Do you address your pastor as Michelle or Pastor Washington? I'm pretty sure you put some respecK on their names and address them by their respective titles, right? Right! On that note, why do you call your Worthy Matron by her first name? Why do you address other sisters in the Chapter by their first names? According to page 18 in your Ritual, female members of this Rite are called Sisters, and males are called Brothers. Please put some respecK on their names as well!

I challenge all of you who fit the criteria to trade in all that hatred, jealousy, animosity, and bitterness for some love, class, dignity, and morals. Let's learn to love one another and be Sisterly. The Order of the Eastern Star is an illustrious, not lustful organization so let's join hands and hearts and bring Order in the Order. We are Fairest among Thousands ALTOGETHER Lovely.

Black women, we are the salt of the earth, the birth of civilization, before us there were none and after us, there will be no more. On the flip side, we are the most hated and disrespected group of people, why? Because everyone envies us. What I don't understand is how we can expect others to love and respect us when we don't even love and respect ourselves.

Look at them white girls getting injections so they can get big butts and thick lips like black women. Are tanning booths for people who want to bleach their skin? They're even getting hair weave so they can have braids and locks like us.

Do y'all realize how valuable we are? We have melanin in our skin that's worth millions of dollars, far more than diamonds and gold. Why do you think we're being killed and kidnapped every day?

Don't think it's a coincidence that our organs are missing before we reach the morgues.

Look at Henrietta Lacks, her cells outlived her and have cured many diseases. They were used in the Covid-19 vaccine, polio, chemotherapy, and AIDS just to name a few. She's the only person in the world whose cells reproduce indefinitely. Scientists have said that if all her cells (HeLa) were put together, they could circle the equator three times and would outweigh 100 Empire State Buildings. That's how powerful we as Nubian Queens are, despite what the world says about us and what we think of ourselves.

I mentioned our Melanated sister, Dr. Gladys West earlier, she invented the GPS that we can't live without today. Some of us used to get lost trying to find our way across the street.

Dr Patricia Bath was the first Melanated woman to receive a medical patent. She invented the Laserphaco Probe used to remove cataracts from the eyes to prevent blindness. If it weren't for her, I wouldn't be writing this book because child, I had cataracts removed from my eyes. I was well on my way to reading in braille so once again, thank you, Dr. West.

In 1966, our Melanated sister, Mrs. Marie Van Britton Brown invented the alarm systems, without her, there would be no Ring cameras or ADT.

On December 23, 1919, our Melanated sister, Mrs. Alice Parker invented a natural gas and heating system that eliminated the need for wood and coal used for wood-burning furnaces in our homes. She's the reason I survived the first 19 years of my life in Rockford Illinois AKA the North Pole.

On July 14, 1885, our Melanated sister, Mrs. Sarah Good invented the Murphy Bed. In

1972, our Melanated sister, Mrs. Shirley Chisholm became the first woman Presidential Nominee. She was also a member of Delta Sigma Theta Sorority. Shout out to the ladies in the red dresses with their trunks up! We can't forget our ancestor Ms. Barbara Jordan, the first Melanated Congresswoman from the Deep South and the first woman elected to the Texas Senate.

Our Melanated sister, Mrs. Harriet Tubman, the Moses of her people, risked her life trying to free thousands of her enslaved brothers and sisters and said she could've freed thousands more if they had known they were slaves (LMAO). That's what I call sisterhood!

Melanated women have made significant contributions throughout history. I can go on for days telling of the mighty works and contributions of our sisters, not to mention the inventions that were stolen from them or just ignored in history.

Have y'all ever seen Hidden Figures? Those sisters made me proud, but honey, every time I think about Octavia Spencer's pie in The Help, she's the real MVP.

I said all that to say that we don't have to walk through life showing our titties and asses trying to be relevant. Esther won the world's first beauty pageant and was coronated Queen wearing a white robe! Somebody please give Lizzo that memo and tell her the minstrel show is over.

We weren't born to be bitches and hoes; we descend from a royal lineage of kings and queens so let's straighten our crowns and claim our position on the throne. We have natural beauty inside and out.

As Melanated women, we have been through hell and back but still, we rise. We've awakened in the morning sitting on top of the world, but by the time we go to bed at night the world is sitting on top of us but still, we rise.

Society is quick to call ourselves and our Melanated Kings criminals because of the color of our skin, but truth be told, the most egregious and contemptible crimes committed on AmeriKKKan soil were not committed **by** our Melanated Kings but **against** them! I can go from A-Z several times and each letter will expose a crime committed against us! If you want to discuss it further, meet me at Johnny Boys Ribs in Oscarville Georgia. If you're not familiar with Oscarville, please google it.

Mrs. Anna Mae Beasley, the Uber driver just revealed to me that she's a Past Grand Matron, then she abruptly pulled her car over. I laughed because when she hit the curb, the 8-track cassette went off and the windshield wipers came on. I thought she was getting ready to straighten my crown or kick me out of her '67 Pinto. Instead, she told me that she agreed with everything I said and that she had been feeling this way for a long time but was scared to voice her opinion for fear of retaliation. I told her that I was not afraid of retaliation or retribution because The Most High follows me where he leads me and only a hit dog will holler.

In conclusion, sisters, let's work on ourselves. I stand accused of being imperfect, The Most High is still working on me. I didn't mean to offend anyone but how things are being done, some of y'all probably didn't realize it's disorderly. All due respect to the elders who might be reading this book, I'm sorry for my language, I don't apologize for anything I said but I'm sorry y'all had to read this. I'm sure my mother is turning flips in her grave because I was raised better than this, but I feel it needed to be said, sorry Momma.

In the name of the departed heroines whose virtues we strive to emulate, I plea with y'all to do everything in your power to bring Order in the Order. Let's keep our white robes unspotted from the ruins of the world. Don't let the things going on around you get inside of you. Our bodies are our temples so let's keep them clean, decent, and in order.

After driving for 357 hours, we finally made it to Houston. What a drive huh! I still can't believe this raggedy-ass pinto didn't break down on us. I'm tired, my knees and back are sore, and to make matters worse, I'm hungry. I think I will stop by my favorite food truck, Soul Goode on Westheimer Rd. My mouth is watering for some of that fish, cabbage, macaroni, yams, and cornbread. My Gawd, it ought to be against the law for food to be this good. It's so good I wish I could throw it up and then eat it again. LoL, I know that sounds disgusting but I'm just saying.

Thanks again for your purchase and I hope you were enlightened and not enraged.

With Love, Past Worthy Matron Tanya Rice.

ABOUT THE AUTHOR

Tanya Rice is the youngest of 11 children and the mother of two sons. She is originally from Rockford IL but now resides in Houston TX. She graduated from the University of Houston Downtown with a bachelor's degree in criminal justice. In her spare time, she loves to read, travel and ride her Can-Am Ryker.

She has been a member of the Order of the Eastern Star for 26 years and is a Past Worthy Matron. Her passion for reading and her diligent research over the past 26 years is what inspired her to write this Study Session.

In her own words, "There's is too much information packed in here to be a book or a study guide!" Which is why she coined it a Study Session.

Made in the USA
Columbia, SC
15 June 2024